INMATES' SURVIVAL HANDBOOK

An Islamic Perspective

Sidney Rahim Sharif, Imam

authorHOUSE®

AuthorHouse™
1663 Liberty Drive, Suite 200
Bloomington, IN 47403
www.authorhouse.com
Phone: 1-800-839-8640

First published by AuthorHouse 9/30/2008

ISBN: 978-1-4389-0244-9 (sc)
ISBN: 978-1-4389-0245-6 (hc)

Printed in the United States of America
Bloomington, Indiana

This book is printed on acid-free paper.

CONTENTS

FORWARD

(Introduction)

Crime and Corrections, an Islamic Perspective is the title of a book I wrote in *1982*. The concerns expressed then about the rapid growth of prison populations in America is still very much a concern today. According to latest statistics published by the United States department of justice, there are *6,996,500* men and women under correctional supervision. Of this number *4,151, 125* are on probation; and 765, 355 are paroled; *713,990* are in jail and *1,421,911* are in state and federal prisons. It appears negative influences are stronger today and they are producing criminals while encouraging antisocial behavior more than ever before.

This book placed more emphasis on the disproportionate African-American prison population. This population ratio still represent a larger number of inmates than any other group in America. I am well aware of injustices African Americans suffer due to racism. Poverty, ignorance; and the negative impacts of racism are causal factors in the growing African American prison population. It is clear however, that racism is not the only variable causing these disproportionate numbers.

This race also has emotional and psychological social problems that can lead to early adult incarceration. The following study demonstrates this theory; .A psychiatrist by the name of Kenneth Clarke along with his wife Mamie, using dolls, produced a landmark study of children. Beginning in *1939* Dr. Clark and his wife conducted tests in which they presented Black and White children with black and white dolls. The children asked to decide which of the dolls were "nice" and which were "bad." Overwhelmingly, white and black children favored the white dolls. When black children were asked which doll they preferred, they invariably chose the white doll. They said it was a good doll and the Black doll was the bad one. Black children, while looking at themselves in a mirror said they were bad.

Clark's study helped persuade the Supreme Court to strike down segregation in the case of Brown versus the Board of Education; this case gave stark proof of the emotional harm that the practice of segregation was doing to black children.

("Separate but equal" was not working.) One writer said you might determine a lot about a child from the way she plays with her doll. This study tells us, without ambiguity, that black children were not very proud of their appearance or color. How can one have confidence in him/herself when they do not like themselves? I remember a great social reformer once asserting. "The black man in America is the world's worst hater of self."

Maybe it is hatred of self and his/her race that causes one to turn against themselves and those of the same likeness. *(If you do not like yourself, this makes it easier for you to dislike or injure yourself or similar looking people.)* How else can we explain the following statistics? In the year *2004, 14,121* Americans were murdered. Of these *6,632* were African Americans who constitute about *12%* of our nation's population.

African Americans represented *47%* of the nation's murder victims and these are primarily Black on Black crimes. In addition, to this number of African Americans killed, more than one in four was 21 years old or younger. Because of repeated murders in most African-American urban communities, death by violence is no stranger. In these places, some children can tell you what its like to pass by corpses on the way to school. In places like these, life is hard and money is tight. Most of the children in these places do not have a father or a man in the home. Many children in these places cannot name their father. (His name is not on the child's birth certificate) In neighborhoods like these, youngsters strut about with the "look tough ghetto shuffle" that often comes with a gun in the pocket. In addition, most of them know the words to the latest violence oriented filthy rap song or video.

In places like these, death becomes a way of life, a lesson that young people learn quickly. How often have we heard about drive-by shootings causing the death of the young unintended victims? Most of these drive-bys occur in densely populated African American neighborhoods in every major city in America.

Caucasians rarely drive through densely populated African American neighborhoods to do "drive-bys." Many years ago white men did perform occasional "drive-by" shootings in African American neighborhoods, during the days of the Ku Klux Klan. And often the local sheriff accompanied them *(Thank God most of those days are over.)*

Most "drive-by's" today are limited to Black on Black perpetrators. It often appears that African Americans are hell bent on wiping each other out. Poverty, racism and ignorance are variables that have contributed greatly to the inability of many African-Americans to lead normal lives. These variables must be considered, when addressing problems and offering solutions to help African-Americans re-establish their communities and themselves with morality and dignity.

I am familiar with the "Caucasian Conspiracy against the Black man theory." I have listened to African Americans say that Caucasians have collectively conspired to introduce and maintain illicit drugs in their communities. According to their conspiracy theories, this plan was implemented by White folks in order to keep Black people mentally sedated while involved in drug trafficking and other criminal activity.

However, I have yet to see a Caucasian or group of Caucasians enter an African American community, over power its people and forced them to use drugs.

In this book, I emphasize my belief that the incarcerated need spiritual guidance in their efforts to reconcile their relationship with themselves and God. (This requires inmates to become God conscious.) This perspective may help inmates get past negative concerns they may have about racism.

You cannot make people love you or like you. However, you can begin to respect yourself and develop an appreciation for yourself. I stress the need for the individual to become more God conscience in his quest to reconcile the difference between right and wrong. After reconciling these differences and re-building their character on a morally strong foundation, inmates can begin to govern them selves accordingly. While my writings continue high lighting the African American prison population and its causes, I am addressing the needs of all inmates regardless of race, color, nationality or creed.

I believe most inmates are concerned about their personal lives, fellow inmates, families, communities and their country. There are inmates that feel helpless and hopeless. They feel too far removed to receive or give help from their families. Because, of their emotional state, some feel unable to make spiritual or social connections that could help themselves and their loved ones.

I believe in the human spirit that we all possess through, Allah (Gods) grace. This spirit will always lift our expectations for hope and remove the sense of hopelessness that manifests its self in too many inmates. I hope and pray that others will benefit greatly from reading this book. It emphasizes the importance for inmates to seek knowledge while serving time. The difference in people is knowledge and when applied it can produce a sense of empowerment.

I do advocate Islam as a way of life but this is not an effort to seduce one to accept a religion. Its an effort to help readers think positive about themselves. In addition, I believe it will help readers improve their self-actualization and offer themselves another choice.

I have found when studied with understanding, Islam can help us make better choices and one of the best methods of learning Islam, is to read the Quran. Islam is an Arabic word. When translated from Arabic to English, Islam simply means the surrender or submission to Almighty God. Muslim is an Arabic word. When translated from Arabic to English, Muslim describes anyone or anything that submits to God. This is a noun. The Sun submits to God. Therefore, the Sun is Muslim by definition. According to the Qur'an, which is God's revelation to man, Allah says that He created everyone and everything Muslim. Simply put, everything in creation was made by God and it submits to Him.

Criminal justice scholars, public policy makers, and others have concluded that America cannot build itself out of this dilemma of crime and incarceration. Yet, most of our national, state and local leaders are politically motivated to continue building prisons in efforts to relieve us of this dilemma. Crime, public safety, and security are good political "hot buttons". If you are "a good politician" and you want to be re-elected, your message to your constituency will be a strong stand against crime. Your position would probably be, "if you do the crime you must do the time".

There is another way. Let us reduce both crime and recidivism

SOMETHING ABOUT THE AUTHOR

The author Sidney Rahim Sharif was born in *1934* in Memphis, Tennessee. His family moved from Memphis to Chicago, Illinois in *1944*. Sharif became involved in the criminal justice system in *1959* after joining the Chicago Police Department. He remained a police officer for 28 years and during this time, he reverted to Islam. In *1969*, he became the first Chicago police officer to accept publicly the religion Islam. While a police officer, he was a longtime observer of the criminal justice system especially at the usual point of entry for the accused.

His duties included foot and beat car patrol on the streets of Chicago. He participated in emergency medical transportation assignments, and ultimately became a detective in *1965*. He worked as a robbery detective *(investigator)*. Two years later in *1967*, he was transferred to the newly formed gang intelligence division and worked in this capacity until *1983*. In *1975* Imam Sharif began his Islamic missionary work in the Cook County Jail. While visiting inmates, he would teach the pillars of faith to anyone who would listen. He soon began teaching Islam in Illinois state prisons such as Menard, Statesville and the Dixon, Illinois Correctional facility. In addition, he counseled inmates and taught Islam in the federal jail located on Van Buren and Clark Streets in Chicago. He made visits to the Federal Prison in Marion Ill. *(One of the first "super maximum security prisons built in the U.S.)*

In *1983*, he was assigned the position of executive security officer for Mayor Harold Washington *(the first African-American mayor in the history of the city of Chicago)*. In 1988, he resigned from the Police Department and in *1989*, he was appointed as Director of Security for Malcolm X College *(a city college of Chicago)* He worked in this capacity for five years.

In *1995* Imam Sharif and his newly acquired wife Sister Esther D. Sharif founded the South Shore Islamic Community Center in Chicago located at *2672 E. 75th Street*. This location was formerly a tavern named, the Birdcage Lounge. The establishment of this institution afforded the Sharif's an opportunity to work with "at risk youths" in the neighborhood. South Shore Islamic Community Center soon became a show place promoting positive community activities and values among the attending youth. The center soon became a neighborhood island of peace for many children before and after school hours. In addition, we worked with youths who were on probation through the juvenile courts enabling them to perform community service.

Jumah *(Friday)* prayers were conducted at the center and Taleem *(teaching and learning sessions)* were held on Sundays. During summer months, the Center offered free lunches to school-age children, their parents, and anyone else requesting food.

In *1999*, Sharif moved his family to Tucson, Arizona. In the year 2000, he begin working for the Pima County Juvenile court as a Juvenile probation officer. While working in this capacity he began serving as a volunteer Imam and counselor at the Arizona State prison in Tucson. Sharif continues to work in this capacity and he prays that Allah continue blessing him with the strength to maintain a presence at this location. Sharif prays that when he can no longer work in this capacity, others will step forward to continue the mission.

Sharif was educated in Chicago, Illinois completing his college education while serving as a police officer. He is a graduate of the University of Illinois at Circle Campus where he acquired his B.A. degree in the administration of Criminal Justice. He subsequently attended and graduated from the Chicago State University earning his M. S. degree in Corrections and the Administration of Criminal Justice.

ACKNOWLEDGEMENTS

I give all honor and praise to Allah (God) and I bear witness that His last Messenger is Prophet Muhammad. I pray that His choicest blessings are granted to His last Messenger. I thank Him for blessing me with my family and parents Dudley C. and Grace J. Clark. For, without them I would not be here to write this book. I thank my loyal lovingly dedicated wife and help mate Sister Esther D. Sharif, for her patient assistance and support. I thank all Criminal Justice Institutions and its public servants for the respect they have demonstrated towards Muslim inmates and in general the religion of Islam. I thank all Muslims who dedicate their time servicing inmate prison populations. And, lastly I thank our prison inmate populations for their historical respect and support they have extended Muslims inmates over the years in America.

SHAITAN OR THE (DEVIL)
By Imam Sidney R. Sharif

The Devil (Shaitan) is real and He has strong appeal.

However, He has no power except in the trickery He wields.
He beckons everyone all of the time, and if you respond to Him, He will regulate your mind.

His power of suggestion is greater than you think; and He can trick you before your eyes blink.
When you do something stupid and you don't know why.
You can rest assured the Devil is standing by.

If you are not satisfied with being your natural self, the Devil will encourage you to become something else.

When you decide that you would rather lie and steal, guess who will show you how to really deal?
When you think you are better than others, because of your looks, your wealth, or your fame; the Devil has made you a part of His game.

Play on Player. But remember; you are being played.

"WE SEEK REFUGE WITH ALLAH (GOD) FROM THE REJECTED DEVIL."

CHAPTER 1
INMATES HAVE THE RIGHT TO STUDY ISLAM

I recommend every inmate study Islam. You have a right to learn this way of life and I encourage you to do so. When studying this "way" it will provide you with a broader philosophical perspective. In addition, it will enable you to "think out side of the box". Everyone has a right to know about this significant "way". Rational human beings must be able to think for themselves and make decisions about what behavior is fundamentally best for themselves and others.

The choice to reject Islam should be yours and not someone else. Before beginning your studies, you should ask yourself the following questions. Why do many Americans avoid studying this subject? Is avoidance fear induced, or ignorance? Why does America's main stream media, offer disproportionate numbers of negative images *(stories) and comments about* Islam compared to other religions such as Christianity and Judaism?

I have heard the following false arguments against studying Islam. "If you start fooling around with Muslims, they will brainwash you or you will brainwash yourself, or this is the devils religion. Islam is a Black religion and its' not for Caucasians. These arguments suggests an individual doesn't have the sense to study a subject without it having a negative effect, or one doesn't have the capacity to make sound decisions for them selves. They also suggests that one may become hexed or have a spell cast on them by some invisible force.

Inmates are humans and God gave inmates the same rights to life and liberty and the pursuit of happiness given to others. I encourage everyone, including inmates to pursue knowledge, study Islam and other subjects in search of wisdom. Do not be afraid to stray from your normal path of understanding. You can always return. There is no harm in you exploring and possibly finding a new way that best suit you. Do not allow yourself to be trapped mentally and emotionally by a needless fear of the unknown

You will learn that Prophet Muhammad *(PUBH)* enjoins men and women "to seek knowledge from the cradle to the grave." Seek knowledge even if you have to go to China."

Prophet Muhammad lived his life according to way prescribed by God. God according to the Quran, said that Prophet Muhammad was sent to the world as a Mercy and a healing. Muhammad's life was designed by Allah, and *his* life serves as a model or pattern of behavior for all men and women. What prevents us from "doing unto others, as you would have them do unto you?" "You are to want for your brother or sister that which you want for yourself."

Prophet Muhammad, (peace be upon him), teaches the following to all people "if a man educates his daughter he is guaranteed paradise". Why are women and girls in some "Islamic" societies beaten and mistreated when they attempt to attend school or learn to read when over *1,400* years ago, under the leadership of Prophet Muhammad *(PBUH)*, women were voting, choosing their leaders and running their own businesses in the cities of Mecca and Medina in Arabia.

There are many excellent books available for you to study about the life of Prophet Muhammad. You do not have to be a "wise scholar" before studying Islam. Remember, the Quran (the holy book of Islam) was revealed to an unlettered prophet. The Quran is your revelation from God through the agency of Prophet Muhammad.

There is no law against studying Islam in prison. More important, God enjoins you to "seek knowledge." Read the Quran, it will lead you to knowledge. I have found that most prisons do not allow inmates to attend Islamic services, unless they declare themselves Muslims. However, this rule does not apply to inmates seeking to attend Christians services. To put it another way inmates do not have to declare themselves Christians in order to attend other religious services.

Among many inmates, a stigma is associated with Islam. Islam teaches us there are evil spirits or influences that cause many to flee from that which is good in pursuit of that which is indecent. *(The Devil is a wicked mind that struggles to lead humankind away from God's path).* The Devil's aim (*THE ARCH DECEIVER*) is to frighten you a way from your blessing. You must set your on standard and not allow yourself to be coward down.

I find this stigma amusing because there's no stigma or negative connotations attached to inmates reading pornographic books. You can study the art of prostitution, gang banging, black power, white power, Christianity, Judaism, Atheism, Satanism warmongering, arms manufacturing, homosexuality, child pornography, domestic violence, illicit drug use, without raising any eyebrows. Why are you afraid to ask a fellow inmate to discuss Islam? What do you have to lose? You should be a little curious.

I urge the reader cultivate the courage that God has given you. Do not be intimidated by ignorance or ignorant people. If you do not want others to recognize your curiosity or your quest to study Islam (the way), this is understandable. Most inmates live in emotionally volatile and sometimes hostile environments. You must be cautious. Many cannot handle the message of Islam and may turn on you without warning. Perhaps they are emotionally unstable. Prophet Muhammad (pbuh), suffered similar hostilities. (According to a recent study, one out of five prison inmates have serious emotional problems.)

If you are afraid to study Islam, you are not alone in your fear. The US government fears Islam. Some of our governments' leaders expressed fear of Islam after the collapse of The Union of the Soviet Socialist Republic. After the Russian republic fell apart, many Eastern European countries regained their freedom and independence. They were no longer under the paw of the Big Russian Bear.

Some of our "wise leaders" fabricated a big lie by stating, "Our next enemy is Islam." We should ponder on this assertion. Why should Islam be viewed as our enemy when it represents a peaceful way of life? How can my desire for peace be a threat to others?

Islam answers the following questions. How am I supposed to live my life as a human being? What is a human being, and how does he/she manage their affairs? What is the human beings relationship to God and his fellow human beings? How am I to relate to my family, my neighbors, my friends and community? We are taught some of these social standards as children and later we learn in schools, relationships, and universities. However, as we mature, we find that some of things that we have learned and begin executing, were not correct nor designed to protect our best interest.

What caused some people to go astray, even though they have good intentions? Human beings need a guide or a manual to live by. We need guidance to operate our lives just as we need a manual to operate a computer, automobile or washer dryer. Which is the most dangerous to operate, a human being, your automobile or rocket ship? A human being, without God's guidance, is a menace to himself and others.

Man is too emotionally fragile to survive, as a human being, without spiritual protection and guidance from God.

When you stand accused of a crime, our courts do not accept a "not guilty plea" based of the defense of "the Devil made me do it." But, we know false ideas and desires can cause men/women to harm themselves and others. False ideas and concepts produce false realities. The Quran is your manual, Prophet Muhammad *(PBUH)* is your Instructor, and Allah is the author and designer of all creation including yourself. Do you think that He would place you in this Earth without Guidance?

"When trouble touches man he cries out to us in all postures-lying down on his side, or sitting, or standing. But when We have solved his trouble, he passes on his way as if he had never cried out to us for a trouble that touched him!! Thus do the deeds of transgressors seem fair in their eyes?" *(Qur'an S.10 –A.12)*

CHAPTER 2
WHAT DOES ISLAM MEAN?
WHAT IS IT?

"Islam simply means the submission or surrender to God." In its ethical meaning Islam signifies "striving after the ideal." The word Muslim translated from Arabic to English defines anything or anyone who submits to the will of God. Therefore, by definition the Sun, Moon and stars are Muslim. Why? Because they are a part of God's creation and they must submit to His will. Hence, these heavenly bodies are Muslim. The words Salaam and Muslim are derived from the word Islam. In the traditional Muslim greeting of As Salaamu Alaikum , the greeter is wishing or praying that Gods' peace will be yours. Islam offers hope of salvation to the righteous and God-fearing of all religions.

Muslims believe in divine revelations of all named and unnamed Prophets in Bible, Torah and Quran. These men

"RANGE FROM ADAM THROUGH MUHAMMAD". These Prophets of course include Abraham (the up right one), Jesus and the final Prophet Muhammad (pbuh) Islam does not accept that God assumed human form. The Quran, Muslims believe, is God's Word and final revelation to Prophet Muhammad for all times and for all human beings.

The following hadiths, (sayings) or quotations are the pronouncements of Prophet Muhammad: "The first thing created by God was the intellect."

"The most excellent Jihad is that for the conquest of self."(The fight or struggle against the rebellious spirit within ones' self.)

"The ink of the scholar is worth more than the blood of the martyr."

"One learned man is harder on the devil than a thousand ignorant worshipers."

"Reflect upon God's creation but not upon his nature or else you will perish."

"Riches are not from an abundance of worldly goods, but from a contented mind."

"He who wishes to enter paradise at the best door must please his mother and father."

"No man is a true believer unless he desires for his brother that which he desires for himself."

"When a funeral procession passes by whether it is a Jew, Christian or Muslim rise to your feet."

"The thing which is lawful, but disliked by God, is divorce."

"Modesty and chastity are parts of the faith"

"Heaven lies at the feet of mothers"

"Actions will be judged according to intentions"

"That which is lawful is clear, and that which is unlawful is clear, but there are certain doubtful things between the two from which it is well to abstain".

"The proof of a Muslim's sincerity is that he pays no attention to that which is not his business."

"That person is nearest to God, who pardons…him who would have injured him."

"Yield obedience to my successor, although he may be an Abyssinian slave".

"Assist any person oppressed whether Muslim or none Muslim."

"The creation is like God's family, and the most beloved onto God is the person who does well for God's family."

The above "hadiths" (sayings or quotes) from Prophet Muhammad are just a few of thousands that were recorded by his companions during his life time.

Islam is a unifying way of life that does not exclude anyone because of race, nationality, or tribe. Its message is inclusive and this inclusiveness is unconditional. Allah (God) says "He created all men Muslims." In the traditions of Islam, social friction because of differences is limited whenever possible. Social friction is usually the product of avarice, vindictiveness, jealousy and lies. In addition, social friction often develops, because of envy, which in turn can create enmity and divisiveness. This is unacceptable.

America has a unique pluralistic society. Unlike other countries our social divisions follow various lines. Pluralism makes our country unique in its social composition and it represents one of Americas' greatest strengths. This social composition is also a part of our prison societies. America's prison societies are equally pluralistic however they are clearly divided. These divisions are enhanced because of ignorance, the lack of space, and prison policies due to security concerns.

Within prison societies we have Democrats, Republicans, independents, liberals, skinheads, African Americans (with their various gang affiliations) White Power advocates, Southern Mexicans, northern Mexicans, Columbians, Christians, Jews, Muslims, Wickens and Native Americans. I urge inmates and others to think about the decisions they make while interacting with their fellow human beings. Why do you dislike a person because they are a part of another racial group? What causes this distain for ones fellow human being? Islam the surrender or submission to God is a way of life that requires us to think seriously about what we do and why.

71. Say: "Oh people of the book! You have no grounds to stand upon unless you stand fast by the Law, the Gospel, and all the revelation that has come to you from your Lord." It is the revelation that cometh to thee from Thy Lord, that increase in "most of them they're obstinate Rebellion and blasphemy. But sorrow thou not over these people without faith."

72. "Those who believe in the Quran, those who follow the Jewish scriptures, and the Sabians and the Christians, Any who believe in God and the Last Day, And Work Righteousness, on them shall be no fear, nor shall they grieve." Quran chapter 5 verses 71-72.

WHAT DO MUSLIMS BELIEVE?

Muslims have six fundamental beliefs. These include the five pillars or principals of faith. Muslims believe in life after death. (Death does not allow one to avoid the consequences of their deeds while living.) We believe in the angels of God.

Angels are forces in nature created to perform tasks ordered by God. (Angels are obedient to their Creator. They do not question their orders nor do they hesitate in executing them. Muslims believe in the seen as well as the unseen. We believe in reward and punishment. (After physically dying, we believe all men/women will be resurrected and rewarded by God, after judgment day for the deeds they have performed.) The Muslim believes that his life, his death, his services and sacrifices are all for Gods pleasure. The Muslim believes that Allah (God) has no partners. He has no son or associate. Jesus is not the son of God. This is not to deny Prophet Jesus status as one of God's Messengers. However, he is not God nor is he to be associated with God. Praying to Jesus- as if he is God- is an unforgivable sin. Muslims do not believe that you can use Jesus or any person as a mediator between you and Allah.

FIVE PILLARS OF FAITH

The religion of Islam is based on five pillars of faith. To understand the concept of five pillars let us visualize the construction of a building or the raising of a tent.

The first pillar is the acceptance of Allah (God) as the absolute ruler and author of creation and the acceptance of Prophet Muhammad as His last and final Prophet and Messenger.

The second pillar of faith is Prayer (Salat). Every able bodied Muslim (believer) is obligated by God to pray five times daily at prescribe times.

The third pillar of faith is Charity or (Zakat). Charity is an obligation from Allah.

The forth pillar of faith is fasting during the month of Ramadan. (Ramadan is the ninth month in the lunar calendar.)

The fifth and final pillar of faith is the Hajj (Pilgrimage). Every adult who is financially and physically able to do so is obligated to perform the Hajj. The hajj entails the believer traveling to Mecca at a prescribed time and performing certain rituals ordained by Allah through His Messenger.

The five pillars of faith have profoundly significant spiritual values. These values (principles) are designed by Allah, for the benefit of all men/women for all times. When these pillars are accepted, understood and implemented, people of faith, will find them selves in a state of Islam. (Surrender or Submission to God) Prophet Muhammad (Peace Be Upon Him) is God's last messenger and as such all men and women have been instructed by God to pattern their lives after him. There is a common saying among some; "as a man thinks so he is".

Chapter 3
Prison Is Not A Fun Place

I have interviewed and talked with many inmates and ex-offenders. I have questioned them about recidivism. I have asked them how they feel about re entry into society and why. Some have told me that after their release from prison, they found it too difficult to make it on the "outs" and they purposely break the law in order to return to prison. This is an observation of which the public is unaware. The average person would never think that a man recently released from prison would want to return to because it is too difficult for him to establish himself as a free civilian.

I have also talked with current and former inmates who expressed genuine anxiety and apprehension about returning to prison upon their release. They do not plan to return to prison under any circumstances. In addition, some ex-offenders have advice for those who have never gone to prison as well as for those who are engaged in criminal activity that may lead them into prison.

While riding an interstate bus, I over heard an interesting conversation between two young adults. (Male and female) While listening to the conversation, it became obvious to me that they knew each other and had lived in the same neighborhood. The young man began inquiring about who was "working on the corners". He mention names of certain individuals and she responded by telling him whether or not the persons named were still actively engaged in criminal activities such as drug peddling, gang banging or had gotten busted etc.

The young man, after learning of those who had become active drug dealers and those recently arrested, made the following statement. "I had recently gotten out of the joint a few days ago and I learned that the police are not playing." He said repeatedly "the five 0" (This is a term used to identify local police officers.) is not playing and that they were going to put every one of those brothers in the joint. The young man confessed that he has been out of circulation because he "caught a case" and he did not really know what was currently happening on the street.

In essence, he said that he has seen the light and was through with all the "dumb stuff". He said that going to prison is not a fun experience for him and it is not a good place to be. His friend responded saying "the way some of the fellows talk about prison life, they make it appear that going to prison can be a lot of fun". The young man retorted. "Believe me Sister that is a bunch of B.S. When you go to prison in Texas you are literally returning to slavery".

Those white guards are going to "Dog" you out. You will do hard labor on farms as if you are a slave, and they will kick your ass if you get out of line. You will be addressed as niggers and any other name they can think of. You will not get enough food to eat, its' not the best food in the world, and those guards will work you all day. This young man looked to be about 21 to 25 years of age. He was neatly groomed, expressed himself intelligently, and he wore causal clothing that young men wear during the summer months.

I can easily relate to some of the things that this couple discussed. They had apparently lived in the Dallas-Fort Worth urban area, and some of us are familiar with the Texas prison system. Texas is one state that makes no bones about corrections. The Texas penal system is not about correcting behavior it is about punishment. "You do the crime you do the time". When it is all said and done, the Texas penal system is a reflection of all of your prison systems. Many years ago in the eighteenth century prisons were named penitentiaries. The name has significance.

During the founding of America, prisons were designed after old British or English models. They were supposed to induce a sense of repentance on the part of the inmate. While serving time, criminals were to learn humility, become humble and contrite. They were to become sensitive to the feelings of those whom they had injured and express sincere sorry for what they had done. They were to confess their evils and apologize to their victims or the state. Historically, convicts were imprisoned in order learn how to behave in society, redeem themselves and become repentant. In other words, "say you are sorry and really mean it." When one is truly sorry for a deed they have committed, they can begin to make amends for themselves and others. Are you truly sorry for injuries you caused others or because you were caught? There is a difference. Repentance has to come from the heart.

ATONEMENT

Years ago during the process of teaching convicts the act of repentance, prison wardens or administrators personally greeted each new convict and issued them a Bible and a bucket. Bible's were presented to inmates for study purposes.

By reading the "Good Book," it was theorized that inmates would learn righteousness and Gods way. American prisons were established under the religious values of Christianity. (Good Christian values). The bucket was given to them because that was their toilet. There were no toilets in prison cells at that time.

The concepts of atonement and repentance are very sound and can produce positive results in rehabilitating offenders. The best way to begin an emotional and spiritually healing process is to express regret or sorrow for committing a wrongful deed and to apologize to the victim.

My parents taught us to "behave" and not offend others. And, if we did do something offensive we should apologize to the person offended and refrain from committing the offensive act again. This is a basic universally accepted social lesson. "Do unto others as you would have them do unto you." Our correctional systems must emphasize repentance and atonement in their training models. We often teach inmates anger management and we medicate some in an effort help them control their emotions. Inmates must learn to except responsibility for their choices and behavior. They are imprisoned, as a consequence of their behavior and this lesson must be reinforced at every opportunity.

Most parents teach their children to appreciate the goodness in others and to respect the rights of others. When children enter kindergarten, these parental lessons are reinforced. "Treat others they way you want to be treated."

My parents (May Allah be pleased with them) at an early age taught me how to conduct myself in my home and in public especially if and when I was approached by a police officer. You see there are different rules of engagement for Black youths and white youths when it came to our relationship with local law enforcement officers.

The average White youth often viewed the police officer as his friend while the average Black youth may have been conditioned to fear and distrust the police. You see most black neighborhoods enjoy a different relationship with police officers than white neighborhoods. We can debate the differences in these relationships. They do exist.

"Say; the things that my Lord hath indeed forbidden are: shameful deeds, whether open or secret; sins and trespasses against truth or reason; a signing up partners to Allah, for which He Hath Given no authority; and saying things about God of which you have no knowledge." Quran, Chap. Verse, 33

CHAPTER 4
PRISON GROWTH UNCHECKED

Years ago, I wrote that America did not have the moral strength or the spiritual will to reduce antisocial behavior and thereby reduce its prison population. My argument was/ is that America has grown accustomed to its large prison population because of economics, special interests, and political influences. It is important for inmates and others to understand that government policies are not going to change because some of us think they should. One of my arguments supporting this theory is that we are a nation governed by laws, but laws are not always applied for the greater good. Often times, certain behaviors are legally declared criminal, to assist in controlling the acts of some for the benefit of others. Current U.S. Congressional Mexican and American border proposals can cause one to question the motives of such laws. These groups (stock holders and investors) know that prison growth increases their wealth or influence one way or another.

The goal of these groups (law abiding taxpaying citizens),is an increase in profits at the end of each fiscal quarter, regardless of how it is accomplished. The American public is constantly being fed by manufacturers with often useless products and services, (plasma television sets, cell phones, play stations, clothing etc.) The publics' quest for materialism is the order of the day and this quest for meaningless "toys" is directly related to our increasing prison population. Many people "shop" because it is the thing to do.

Most of our inmates were prosecuted because they were seeking to acquire what is commonly called the "BLING" "BLING". They either went shopping without any money, used a gun, or someone elses drugs or automobile without permission. There are satanic influences in our country's culture, and as I see it, right-mindedness is out of style. We no longer buy because of a need. We buy because we want it.

HERD ANIMALS FOLLOW

Many in our society have adopted the characteristics of herd animals. I believe many young men go to prison following the herd instinct. Without rhyme or reason, they began drifting into a pattern of behavior that will ultimately lead them to the penitentiary. Psychologist have learned, and can predict that antisocial behavior develops during early childhood. Often if this behavior goes unchecked it will lead to un-anticipated consequences.

I do not think Parents intentionally raise their children to populate prisons. However, behavioral scientist can predict with a certain degree of accuracy, when early childhood behavior will lead to incarceration. It has been determined that the more social disadvantages children have such as poverty or having a single mother heading their household who is a high school dropout, the greater their chances of becoming delinquent.

Sociologist have known for sometime that children growing up in physically or mentally impoverishing conditions often do not fair well. Recent studies have now shown that piling up these social disadvantages increasingly magnifies health and other social risk that children may not be able to cope with.

Studies have determined that children having three main social disadvantages such as poverty, low parental education and single-parent households were four times more likely than children were with none of these risk factors to be in poor, fair or good health as opposed to the very good or excellent health.

Children with all three risk factors were twice as likely as children with no risk factors to have a chronic health condition such as asthma and diabetes or mental retardation. Children who have two of the three factors were three times as likely to be in poor, fair or good health then those with none. Youngsters with one risk factor had twice the health risk. These findings appear in the April 2006 issue Of Pediatrics, a journal of the American Academy of Pediatricians.

(The study was conducted by Dr. Ruth Stein, a pediatrician at Albert Einstein College of medicine children's hospital at Montefiore in Bronx, New York.)

Children with the above described a risk factors are also at risk to becoming involved in the juvenile justice system. Because of these risk factors, many children will not finish high school and will ultimately become involved as inmates in juvenile and adult correctional systems.

Our society can annually predict the size of its prison population based on the above studies. But we do nothing to prevent its growth. This complacency suggests we are satisfied with these outcomes or we do not know how to affectively address this problem. There must be some benefits for having the largest prison population in the world. What are they?

1.) For starters, federal, state and local elected officials do not worry about the voting habits of nearly 3 million incarcerated and supervised convicts because they have lost their right to vote. Upon a persons' conviction of a crime in America, they automatically lose their rights as a citizen. This also applies to juveniles on probation. A convict cannot get his rights restored until after he completes his sentence. In addition, he must take the initiative to get his own rights restored. No one is going to do it for him. We must continue processing many of our citizens through the criminal justice systems in order to maintain a significant part of our economy, and to keep our political system functioning. Most cities depend upon state, county and federal monies to keep their local police departments financed.

2.) Our increased prison population helps support a number of community-based organizations through grants and loans for rehabilitation programs. Drug rehabilitation programs, both within and without prisons are now thriving due to an increased and sustained prison population. There is a growing business funded by national and local governments called the prison re-entry program. Citizens are hired through community based organizations, using federal and state grants, to aid ex convicts and paroles. Many of our local towns are primarily financed by prison operations that function within their boundaries. Ancillary businesses both private and public develop and flourish because of growing prison populations. (Prison administrators, correctional officers and their families must have housing, grocery stores, repair shops drug stores etc.)

Communities and towns are currently being built and expanded, due to inmate population growth. Let us not forget that we have over 1,500,000 prison inmates who are (on any given day) getting medical care, food, clothing and shelter paid for by the taxpayers of America. The American taxpayers now pay more for their Criminal Justice System than they pay for public education. (It cost some prisons over 50.00 per day to keep each inmate incarcerated. You do the math.)

3.) Our prison systems are used to replace mental hospitals. One out of five inmates have serious emotional problems. We use our prisons to ease the embarrassing problem of homelessness in the richest country in the world. We use our prisons to furnish housing and health care for forgotten military veterans.

The irony of this situation is that our voting taxpayers continue to vote for an increase in tax dollars for our criminal justice system and refuse to demand support for increases in educational programs such as, pre-school, and early childhood education. A sound public educational system would reduce our criminal justice expenditures while economically strengthening local communities. The rational argument that we should spend more money on public education on the front end to prevent more spending on the back end (the criminal justice system) has become moot.

Our legislators similar to their constituents respond only to emotionally charged "hot buttons". The public is frightened into thinking "we need more police officers and more jails instead of needing more social service programs directed toward human development. We need a pubic health care system and an educational system that addresses the needs of all of our citizens.

The human being is emotionally fragile and without proper guidance, he will self-destruct. If a child does not accept guidance from his parents, it will be very difficult for it to except guidance from others. The lack of guidance and the failure of people to think rationally drives prison growth. Perpetually going to prison, in some cultures, has become as popular as Moms apple pie and Mac Donald's Hamburgers.

Our country has unknowingly cultivated, nurtured and sustained a sizable prison population that will continue growing until the inmates thinking and behavior patterns change. (Over one thousand men/women enter prison daily.

Not only must inmates change their thinking and behavior patterns; our civilian population, which feeds our prison population, must begin to change its way of thinking. Too many American people lack the moral or spiritual strength to control their antisocial behavior. We have a population of approximately 300 million people compared to China with a population of over a billion people. Though we are said to be the wealthiest and most democratic country in the world, we have more people in prison than China or India, which has close to a billion citizens.

At this point in our economic history, it is not in America's best interest to reduce its prison population. Therefore, if the criminal justice system has a life of its own is it feasible for it to curtail its own life? I do not think so. On any given day, America locks down 2.3 million people. Some 656,000 are released every year; and about two thirds of them end up behind bars again. The numbers alone are overwhelming and one has to wonder. What is happening to our society?

"The Devil made me do it ". In Islam, this is a very true statement but it has to be modified. The devil cannot make you do it but he can certainly beckon you.

CHAPTER 4

THE INCREASE IN RECIDIVISM

Asr or Time through the Ages

"By (The Token of) time through the ages, Verily Man is in loss, except such as Faith, do righteous deeds, and (join together) in the mutual teaching of truth, And of Patience And Constancy." (Quran; chapter 103)

There has been a steady increase in our prison population since the establishment of prisons. In 1983, there were approximately 200,000 inmates in our federal and state prisons. Now there are over one million and at least two thirds of these men upon release on parole or after being "maxed out" will return to prison. Some say after being released, the people out there do not give a darn about you. They do not offer you any help and they made it easy for you return to prison. A lot can be said about this. However, on the other side of the coin, another variable needs discussion.

Let us briefly study animals in our nation's zoo's and consider how confinement will alter or affect their natural behavior. Each animal most likely was taken out of its natural habitat and placed in the zoo. The animals removed from their habitats no longer have to concern themselves with their basic needs for survival. All of their needs for survival are made available to them by their keepers. After a while, they learn to anticipate their feeding times, exercise times and petting times. They are no longer under the law of the survival of the fittest. The captured animal no longer concerns itself with trying to capture its prey and loses some capacity to forage for itself. Obtaining food and avoiding dangers presented by other animals is no longer a problem for caged animals. The captured animal has no predator other than its captor and soon develops a sense of security within the confines of its cage or cell.

Most men entering prison find themselves emotionally deflated and devalued by the sudden change. Prison life no longer allows men and women to deal with the day-to-day challenges of living as free men and women in society. (This is not a complaint, this is simply the nature of crime and punishment.) They do not have to worry about paying rent, utility bills, buying food etc. In addition to ones loss of independence and the need for self-reliance, the stigma of being a convicted felon and placed in prison can be a dramatic blow to one's self-esteem.

While administering to some inmates I have learned they have very little self-confidence in their ability to measure up in this world's society. They say they want to be free, they want to get out. However, our statistics tell us that approximately 66% that is 66 out of a hundred people released from prison will return within a two-year period. Some statistics say 75% will return within 14 months.

Once a person has been convicted sentenced and confined, he or she began to rationalize their situation. Here are some of their questions and answers. What did I do that is so wrong? Why am I here? I do not really think I am a criminal. I may have made a mistake but I know many people that have done far worse and they never got arrested let alone went to prison. "Hey after all the President of the United States started a war for no reason, and got a lot of people killed. They did not put Bush in jail.

Inmates began to think a lot about their families while in prison. Some have expressed a love and hate relationship with his or her parents. They think about their close friends running buddies etc.. Some inmates maintain a close relationship with relatives and others do not. Some value their wives, girlfriends and children others do not.

CHAPTER 5
RACISM IN PRISON AND SOCIETY

The simple dictionary definition of racism is ; 1..a belief that one's race is superior. 2. a policy or practice based on racism. The practice of racism in prisons is as prevalent as it is in society. Most people are uncomfortable discussing racism, and I have found many people do not know its definition, or understand its affect on society

Racism, nationalism, and tribalism are some of the tools used by the devil (A Wicked Deceitful Spiritual Influence) and ignorant people to keep men and women in divided. Human races (differences) develop naturally. Tribes and nations are developed naturally. In addition, these attributes of our human existence are attributed to geographical circumstances. Allah (God) "created us in different from one another so that we can get to know each other. Not so that we should despise each other."

People who have lived in certain parts of the world for thousands of years will be physically different in appearance from people who lived in other parts of the world. However these differences do not make any superior to others. The language that one speaks over a period can also alter his facial appearance. If the language that you speak uses a letters sounding B's and Ps, your lips will become fuller than people who do not often use these sounds.

The heat of the Sun will cook you, just as a meat is cooked in the oven. Study the continents of Africa, Asia and Europe you will find that the people who have lived a "these areas for thousands of years, look different from each other. People who live in cold climates have to undergo physical adaptations in order to survive. Pale skin in cold climates enables the human being to stay warmer because the lightness of his skin allows him to reflect Sunrays. The person developing in cold climates will have narrow nostrils. This enables him to protect his lungs from extremely cold air. A lot more can be said about races and how they are developed that this can be studied by the reader on his own time.

Let us suffice it to say that our race does not give us any superiority over another race. In addition, believe me I am not trying to convince you of this fact. You have to study and come to your own conclusions by using the intellect that God gave you. If you believe that, your race makes you superior over another people that is your reality. If your mind is closed to rational and reasonable arguments this is the state that you have to live in.

In Islam racism, tribalism and nationalism must take a backseat. Allah says, "I created you all in the best mold and breathed some of my spirit into you. I created all men/women Muslims and it is their circumstance that caused them to be otherwise."

Men and women will never have a true appreciation for their real worth so long as they labor under the illusion that their race, their tribe or their nation is superior to others.

Inmates have enough problems to deal with while in prison without worrying about their race. As an inmate, you should not waste your energies or your intelligence promoting racism. You should concern yourself with your human survival. Within our prison walls inmates are divided mentally, spiritually, and physically because of racism and nationalism. The Mexicans have their turf, the African-Americans have their turf and the Caucasians have their turf. In addition, within each race or nationality you have your gangs or clubs or groups if you will.

Your rivalry among the races and your gangs are no different from the warring factions that existed when Prophet

Muhammad peace be upon him was growing up in the city of Mecca in Saudi Arabia over 1400 years ago. The peninsula of Arabia was populated and divided by tribes. Each tribe and viewed itself as being superior to other tribes. Just as you strut around the prison yard showing off your tattoos, your hairdos, your muscles and your loud voices so did the tribes of Arabia and other places. I think you know what I am talking about. "Every gorilla thinks he's the biggest until he meets his match."

Racism is a significant factor that aids in keeping a higher ratio of African-Americans imprisoned than other groups. In America, the African-American is still given the short end of a stick by this society when it comes to freedom and justice and equality. For some unexplained reason institutional racism is still very much a part of our society. Let me explain to you just what I mean. If an African-American goes into a bank seeking a mortgage loan, with all things being equal, he will be less likely to get it than a Caucasian. This has been demonstrated time and time again by the Federal housing administration commonly known as FHA. There was a time when very few banks or savings and loans would give an African-American home mortgage loan. Do you own research if you are not convinced.

Time and time again African Americans have been sentenced to death only to find out later that many are not guilty. It is getting so now that it is common to read about an African-American who was falsely imprisoned for years. This tells me that something is awfully wrong and weird about our system of criminal Justice. . I am hoping that African-Americans will come to grips with this reality and stop placing themselves at the mercy of society that is incapable of rendering justice. When we look at this phenomenon, some may declare that our society is racist in nature, based on the outcomes of our death penalty sentencing. Why is there such a disproportionate number of African-American inmates in this country sentenced to death and later declared innocent?

It is very difficult for many young African-American males to accept the reality that many of them have been programmed to enter our criminal justice system. Most of them come from one-parent families and grew up in drug and gang infested communities. In most instances, their parents were born in the same environment. In addition, the young African-Americans who represent over 50% of our prison population come from these communities. They grew up around violence, poverty and apathy. Most of them were not prepared to enter kindergarten. When many African-

American children begin kindergarten, they do not know how to spell their names nor are they able to tell anyone their home address. In New York City over half of its African-American students do not finish high school. In addition, most of these children who did not finish high school have already learned how to sell drugs, commit robberies and burglaries. Many of these children who did not finish high school started experimenting with alcohol and drugs between the ages of eight to 12 years.

Going to prison can be a rite of passage for some young men in African American communities. Many young African American males have family members, friends and community associates who have gone to prison at one time or another. The fathers of these children were probably inmates while they were growing up. Some of these children, through their mother's initiative, visited their fathers while they were in jail. Going to prison may give one bragging rights. How can you say you are tough and have had many life experiences if you haven't gone to jail or prison? You can't be accepted in certain social circles, unless you have "done time." This is the thinking of many young men regardless of race. In these communities, you can't be an effective gang member, if you haven't gone to jail or you are afraid to go to jail.

CHAPTER 6
WHAT INMATES CAN DO TO HELP THEMSELVES AND THEIR FAMILIES

I encourage inmates to communicate with their love ones on a regular basis. I caution them against using the telephone because "you costing your family money". Whether inmates realize it or not their families are concerned about them. They are concerned about their welfare and they would like to hear from them. This is especially true of the children of inmates. Think of the joy you can bring to a child by writing them a letter. Some inmates have younger brothers and sisters who are also struggling to survive in a heartless world. They would love to hear from their brother, uncle, sister, mother or father.

Expressing care and concern for the welfare ones children, regardless of the circumstances is an act of charity. Inmates should communicate with their families on a regular basis by writing. I realize that it is not easy to write letters especially if one is unaccustomed to doing it. Writing can be difficult but yet, it can be very rewarding. Writing to your love ones from a position of strength is definitely an act of charity. When I say write from a position of strength; I mean write encouraging letters. Communicating regularly with family members in a positive way will help both the inmate and their family.

I believe that families are established by God, and God has placed love in the hearts of family members. These are blood ties and they are sacred. The relationship that God has established between you and your family should be held in high esteem.

When you write your family members remember that you are not to complain that things are not going as well as you think they should. Penitentiaries are not designed for your comfort. You were put in prison as punishment, so please do not write complaining about your miseries. If you do, you will immediately "turn people off". Write your family members and tell them that you are in good health and in good spirits. Tell them that you are always sadden when you think about not being there to comfort them.

It is okay to request a visit from your family members. However, make certain that this request is reasonable. If you are requesting that your wife or girlfriend visit you, you have to be conscious of certain realities. If it is your wife no doubt she is struggling to care for herself and for your children. If your children are going to school, their mother "your wife" has to monitor them, comfort them, prepare their meals and clothing. If she is working, she has to take time off from her job to visit you. Can she afford it? Transportation is always expensive, especially when your salary is not that great.

Remember Mr. or Mrs. Inmate; your relative's responsibilities to themselves and other members of their family did not stop when you were sentenced. Whatever you were doing to assist your family when you were free ceased, upon your arrest. The family that you left had to take up the slack. So whenever you are begin feeling "down and out", or "feeling sorry for yourself", think about the situation that you suddenly left your love ones in. One can not understand the plight of another until they try to "putting themselves in their shoes."

Islam teaches us that He Allah Created all men for a purpose and that their purpose is to serve God. He says He Created all men in the best mold, and He put something of His Spirit in them. God goes on to say that "the best of you is the one that is most useful to his community." Even though you are in prison, through God's grace, you have the ability to lift the spirits of others and make them feel good about themselves.

While an inmate, do you recall when you were home with your family? What was your relationship with your family members? Did you encourage your wife or your significant other by telling them that they were a good wife and a good mother or did you make fun of their shortcomings? Did you encourage them to go to school and continue their education? Did you hold them in high esteem or did you esteem them unworthy? Did you encourage your little brother to be a good person, to be a good student in school, and not associate with drug users? Did you encourage him to respect those in authority over him?

The point I am making is this. There are things that you can do to make amends to your family for shortcomings that you exhibited before going to prison. Did you berate your wife or your girlfriend in the presence of your children? Did you physically abuse your wife or girlfriend in the presence of your children? If you are guilty of this past behavior, you may have caused serious psychological or emotional damage to some family members. Your past behavior toward your family could very well be a contributing factor toward your children becoming involved in the criminal justice system. In other words, if you taught them to disrespect their mother by abusing her in their presence, you also taught them to disrespect authority. These seeds of rebellion can blossom into antisocial behavior.

Inmates can comfort their families and friends simply by being sensitive to their needs and their life's challenges. Remember, you have abandoned them. You are no longer there with them but their lives must go on.

Chapter 7
I Want to Be Free

Many men and women leave prison every year. Most of them do not have jobs nor do they have a support system awaiting them in the communities they left. Most inmates, upon their release, lack substantive social connections within their communities. They will say, upon their release that they need and want a job. This concern for employment is significant. Inmates realize that they must be able to earn a living. However when some inmates are released, their behavior is similar to that of an animal suddenly released from a zoo. They may have forgotten how to function in society. Their social skills were perhaps lacking when they were first imprisoned. They may have been unemployable at the time of their incarceration. Unfortunately, these skills are probably still lacking.

There are in house programs designed to help inmates re-enter society upon their release from prison. Counselors are also available, when possible. However, we must realize that employment opportunities for ex-felons are limited. There are, community based agencies that assist in finding jobs for ex-felons and many are successful. After finding a job, the next big challenge for ex- offenders is handling his newfound freedom.

The average inmate or most people for that matter do not realize what freedom is. What does freedom mean? How do you do it? Freedom demands accountability, responsibility and integrity. A human's freedom is not like that of the animal. Freedom suggest that one is capable of making rational decisions or thinking for himself. In other words, the human being is required to think about his behavior and his relationship to others. Allah has given us a free mind. He has allowed us to make choices. But, this does not give us the right to think we can blindly make any choice and not be Censored. Human society is naturally structured, and by its nature, makes demands on each person in society. Animal societies are also naturally structured. Animals cannot deviate from their instinctive nature. The human being is created under natural restraints and by his nature, he lives under internal laws. For example, a ship has a crew and every crewmember has a responsibility to do his job in order to keep the ship afloat. This is why our society teaches its members citizenship. And we should always make certain that each citizen understands and knows the meaning of "citizenship". This word (citizenship) suggests the need for each person to do his or her share to keep society afloat.

The human being does not have the same freedom as that of a dog or any other animal for that matter. The dog and other animals are controlled, and primarily governed by their instinctive nature. The human being is controlled and primarily driven by their ability to think and to reason. Remember the first thing that Allah created was intellect. Human existence dictate that the human think and that his thinking be based in logic and sound reasoning. In America there, was a time when great emphasis was placed on its citizens receiving a quality education and becoming responsible and accountable for their behavior. Our society no longer emphasize the importance of citizen ship and its accompanying responsibilities

Chapter 8

We will pay Whatever It Costs

We live in a society that is willing to spend more money (the taxpayer's money) to put you in prison and keep you incarcerated rather than increase spending to improve education and relieve poverty. Yes, we spend more money in America for prisoner maintenance than we spend for public education. So again, if you are waiting for the public to keep you out of prison because of cost, you will be waiting.

Believe it or not, it cost more money to keep your butt in prison for one year that it costs to pay for a four-year college degree in some universities. Our governments know this and they are willing to pay for it.

This is nothing new. These comparative costs have been discussed for the past 35 to 40 years by policymakers and our state and federal representatives. I am presenting these observations to you as inmates so that you can develop a greater understanding and appreciation for the lifestyle you have chosen.

There is a federal maximum-security prison that is called Super Max, in the state of Colorado. This prison is located near a small town called Florence. It is about 90 miles outside the city of Denver. This prison places every inmate in solitary confinement where he will do his time until he max out or dies. It Cost over $36,000 to keep each inmate in this facility for one year. This particular facility is built in a mountainside below ground level. It has its own hospital, a federal court and everything else needed to maintain and contain its inmates. There is no need to go out side for anything. Each inmate remains in his cell alone 23 hours a day without having contact with anyone else and in addition, the cells are soundproof.

There are many other prisons in Colorado State. Many cities in this state were developed to accommodate prisons. Like many other states, incarcerating people is the engine that drives a percentage Colorado State's economy. If the prison industry in Colorado suddenly went out of business, many of its citizens would be laid off and their home mortgages would be foreclosed.

There is an investment Corp. based in Tennessee that develops private prison systems. The name of this company is

Corrections Corporation of America. In the state of Arizona there is a city named Eloy. This city nearly lost hundreds of jobs at a Privately owned detention center in March 2006. Now this private prison company, CC C and the city of Eloy, Arizona are preparing to open the doors to a new facility and are laying the groundwork for a third prison to open in 2009.

The Correction Corporation of America is planning to host a grand opening of the new Red Rock Correctional Center. A C. C. A. Prison that will house 1596 medium security inmates from Alaska and other states. The $82.5 million Red Rock Center is the company's fourth prison in Pinal county Arizona and it is the second such facility to open in Eloy. This facility will employ about 370 workers and is expected to open July 15, 2006.

With the opening of this prison, Corrections Corporation of America will become the largest employer in Eloy, with more than 630 workers. Eloy's population is about 11,000.

A third CCA owned prison in Eloy, Arizona the Saguaro Correctional Facility, broke ground in May about 100 yards from the red rock Center and is scheduled to open in the year 2007. This facility will house 1896 inmates. It is expected to employ another 400 workers. Eventually the three CCA prison's in Eloy should have a total of 1300 employees with an annual payroll of $50 million according to Mark Brnovich, CCA's senior director of state governmental relations.

For the past 30 years, private industry has invested heavily in building prisons and developing related inmate services. Just as private industry is supporting the military with its military industrial complex and other government projects, it is influencing and supporting the "growth of our prison our industry." Common Citizens who buy stock and wealthy investors who own the stock are betting that the inmate populations is going to continue to increase and investors will become more wealthy.

CHAPTER 9
SEXUAL CHALLENGES IN PRISONS

During incarceration, inmates have to deal with some sense of sexual deprivation. In other words, if you were sexually active before going to the penitentiary you will have to make some serious adjustments. Some prisons do allow inmates to have conjugal visits but most do not.

And, because we live in an environment that promotes sexual promiscuity and applauds sexual prowess, many inmates will have a challenge controlling their sexual urges. Before entering prison, some inmates have been conditioned to think that fornication and promiscuity represents 80 to 90% of their lives. This idea of "sex makes the world go around" is not new in the minds of some and it has become their reality.

I am now recalling an old joke about a hapless dog crossing the railroad track in front of a moving train. While trotting across the track, and not using good judgment, part its tail was cut off by the train's wheels. This was of course a painful experience for the animal. He had lost not only a part of his tail, but some of his dignity.

Instead of licking his wounds and regaining his composure, the dog went back in search of the portion of tail he had lost. While examining this bit of tail, another train came along and severed the poor animals head. The moral of the story should be obvious. "Do not lose your head for a little piece of tail". Inmates beware. I caution you, please be circumspect. Do not allow the dictates of your groin lead you astray.

Remember Mr. or Mrs. inmate be reflective (think). Many of you in prison today because directly or indirectly you were in pursuit of a "piece of tail". You stole a car, robbed the store, stole some drugs or hurt somebody because you were trying to impress yourself or someone else while seeking a cheap thrill. Our marketing industry uses a "little piece of tail" as bait to sell most products.

Who told you that you had to have sex? How did you learn how to have sex? When you were a child, you did not know whether you were a female or a male. You had to learn to be a boy or girl. This means that someone had to teach you. You didn't grow up knowing what to do with your penis or vagina.

There is no law or physical condition that demands one has to engage in sexual relations. Having sex is designed to produce children and propagate the species. Who told you that it is okay for you to poke your prick into another man's butt or his mouth? Who told you "miss lady" that it is OK for you to open your legs and allow anyone too ejaculate in your vagina?

Who told you that the best among you is the one with the biggest "sex organ" or the biggest pair of Balls or Boobs? Now I have a question for some of you big bad muscular and possibly tattooed inmates. (You know who I am talking to.) I am speaking to those who believe it is manly or macho to force a fellow inmate into submission to his insane sexual appetites. My question is this. Who is the pervert, the man who fights to resist a sexual assault or the man who attempts to sexually assault another? Answer that for me Mr. Bad guy. In my judgment, the pervert is the one forcing himself on another person.

It is the devil himself that cause us to think that sex is the most important part of your life. As a child, during your formative years, you have received subtle yet not-so-subtle messages that suggested to you that sexual gratification and the thought of it is the most important part of your life. Recently a television program called dateline USA, conducted a joint sting operation with a local police department.

The sting began with a female police officer posing as a 13-year-old girl trolling the Internet for sexual predators. It wasn't long before she was contacted by a number adult males soliciting whom they thought was a 13-year-old girl. Some of the solicitors, (potential) predators were lured to a home that was staked out by a TV station camera operator and a television producer. Within one hour about 15 adult men, from practically every walk of life, came to the home seeking to have sex with whom they thought was a 13 year old girl. She had told them that she was home alone and that it was okay for them to come in after knocking on the door and announcing themselves.

I cite the above scenario as an illustration of how sexually perverted our society is. Men and women cheapen themselves when they cannot seem to control their biological urges. Human beings were not designed to be ruled by their sexual drives, or their passions and impulses. Sexually Transmitted Diseases (S. T. D.) such as AIDS, HIV, syphilis and gonorrhea are potential threats to the health and welfare of everyone in our society. Because of the physical closeness of individuals in prison, any sex act between inmates will put others at risk.

More over, fear of contracting a sexually transmitted disease should not be the only concern regulating our sexual behavior. Ones genuine fear should be the lack of self-control. We are not animals (in the sense that we are controlled primarily by instinct). As human beings, we are not governed by a mating season, as are animals.

It is a persons artificially induced, perverted sexual appetite that drives one to mate with anything at any time; and if possible anywhere. It is sexual urges of this nature that presents serious problem for some of our inmates. And, our society is unwilling or incapable of solving it. It appears our society encourages and promotes sex acts among its population regardless of age or gender. We do not have to do any more research and studies to determine whether this is true. We have but to look at the behavior of people in our society today. When behavior is centered around sex it appears that nothing is sacred.

This proliferation of bizarre sexual behavior and its public support, under the guise of freedom of speech, causes one to wonder why homosexuality is such a big deal. Since the human being is designed physiologically to mate with the opposite sex to produce offspring, what is the big deal? One of the realities of human existence is this. Human beings do not have to engage in sexual acts in order to enjoy a good quality of life. Human existence entails a lot more than picking a sex mate. The choice is in your hands. If one cannot regulate himself, who can?

Allah says, "He Created men and Jinn for one purpose and that purpose Is to Serve Him".

Chapter 10
The Company We Keep

"Birds of a feather flock together." "When You Lie Down with Dogs You May Catch Flea's". "The Company we keep Has A Lot to Do with Our Character." What company do you keep? Years ago, we said that if you were a good person you would be blessed with friends from all walks of life. But, after giving it some thought, I concluded there are some walks of life with friends I may be better off without. What is a friend?

Prophet Muhammad (made the peace and blessings of a Allah be upon him) says that a believer wants for his brother that which he desires for himself." "A believer will help his brother even if he is in the wrong." Prophet Muhammad was then asked how and why do you help your brother when he is in the wrong? "You help him by holding him back or preventing him from doing wrong".

A friend, in my judgment is someone who is concerned about your welfare, one who will protect you in deed and by precpts. Your first friend of course is Allah the Creator. Your next friend is Prophet Muhammad. Your next best friend is your mother. "A true believer is a mirror to his brother. He protects him from harm." We all have been blessed with various friendships. Some have been helpful, and comforting, especially during difficult times. In addition, I have discovered friends whom I had not previously identified as friends. And, it is important that you understand the difference between a friend and an associate. This can prove to be an important distinction. Some of us are guilty of associating with persons whose behavior was indefensible and embarrassing. If you do not know what indefensible and embarrassing behavior is you should ask a very close relative. Preferably, you should ask your mother, father, grandmother, grandfather, or another who sincerely loves you. Too many of us have suffered the negative affects of associating with "nut cases".

Oftentimes it takes awhile before we can recognize or spot some of our "friends" (Associates). What I mean by this is that it may take awhile before we recognize our true friends. We may think an associate is a friend, though we know very little about him/her. You may or may not identify a friend as a liar until you identified the first lie he tells you. It is the same with a troublemaker or an agitator. Sometimes you may give a person the benefit of doubt. However, when you are alone after dealing with an associate like this you suddenly see them for what they are. We may identify them bluntly as "Hell Raisers, Trouble Makers" etc.

We soon learn that it is "friends and associates" like these that we should avoid, if we want peace in our lives. Remember Mr. inmate it was these kinds of associates and friends that you identified as your "homies" or your family before you went to jail or prison. These are the fellows that you "would go down with." These are the fellows, friends or associates that you depended on to look out for your best interests, and you swore your allegiance to them.

You and many of your "Hommies" are now residing in the same prison. This is something that you need to think about. If you are satisfied with the outcomes (the rewards or results) of your past relationships, you should continue with these associates as you have in the past. Keep the same friends and associates and I will guarantee you that the end results will be the same. In computer language, some say "garbage in garbage out." To put it another way, if you do not want to return to prison after your release, you need to associate with people that think and behave like you. If you consistently associate with someone who is violating the law, you are placing yourself in jeopardy

Prophet Muhammad (peace be upon him) says, "if you feel No Shame Do as You like".

CHAPTER 11
PRISON'S ADMINISTRATIVE ORGANIZATION

Prisons and correctional facilities are state and federally owned institutions. They are financed (supported) by taxpayers and regulated by state and federal laws. They are administratively organized and managed, similar to most large public institutions. It is important for inmates to understand how prisons are designed and managed. Prisons and correctional institutions are semi military organizations, and there is a "chain of command" beginning with the Warden.

The man or woman in charge of your prison carries the title of Warden. The warden is the chief executive officer or (CEO). This person is responsible for overseeing the mission of the prison or correctional facility. The warden has deputy wardens working under his command. They are responsible for managing various units and line personnel (correctional officers) within the prison. Captains, Lieutenants, Sergeants, and ranking COs are usually line supervisors under Wardens and Deputy Wardens.

When a person is found guilty, in a criminal court, they may be sentenced to serve time in a correctional facility. Upon sentencing, the court also orders the warden to accept the convicted person into his custody (prison) and keep him/her there until their time is served. The Warden is not only responsible for receiving you into his or her prison he/she is also responsible for your health, safety and welfare.

The Warden manages his prison similar to how a mayor manages a city. There is a big difference however between the mayor of the city and a prison warden. The mayor was elected by the people. The Warden is usually appointed by the governor. Just as the mayor has, a cabinet that helps him manage the city, the Warden as an administrative staff that assists him or her in managing the prison.

Prisons are not managed, using democratic rules, and a Warden is not obligated to follow democratic principles while carrying out its mission. Inmates seldom see the Warden during their confinement but they do see the correctional officers. Just as the mayor is responsible for his police department, the Warden is responsible for his or her correctional department. Yes, correctional officers represent the police department within the confines of a prison.

In addition, there is very little difference in the mission of police officers and that of correctional officers. Their duties and responsibilities are similar. In fact, the correctional officer's responsibilities, in my judgment, are much more demanding than those of local police officers. For example, the citizen in the city does not normally call the police when he or she has a toothache or needs food. However, in prison in order for an inmate to receive medical care for that toothache or get medical attention, he must report it to the officer on duty.

In reality, whether inmates understand it or not, correctional officers are there for their protection. The correctional officer's duty is to maintain his post in a professional manner and to obey and enforce all applicable laws, rules and regulations. CO's, (correctional officers) are obligated to report or address any infraction of prison rules and regulations. Correctional officers are not watching inmates in order to make them obey the prison laws. Just as your mother could not make you eat if you were not hungry, correctional officers cannot make you follow the prescribed rules and regulations. Often times, one may feel intimidated by an officer's presence, but he is there to remind you of the rules and regulations that govern our behavior. The correctional officers presence serves as the traffic control light that signals one to stop or go. "You are the one driving the car."

Though you are in prison, you still have a choice. (Under the rule of law, human beings must feel and know that they are obligated to obey laws.) Your CO's are there to report you when you violate laws. This is his job. It is his duty and responsibility. He can be cited for dereliction of duty if he fails to report and inmate's indiscretion. The initiative, to follow the rules and regulations governing prison operations, rests solely with the inmates. It is the inmate's responsibility to know the rules and regulations of the institution and to follow them. Correctional officers are not there to force inmates to obey the laws.

When you are free, the same relationship, exist between citizens and police officers. For example, you maybe issued a driver's license, after passing a test. But it is your job, after receiving the privilege of driving, to operate your car in a safe responsible manner. It is not the police officers duty to keep you from speeding. It is his duty to cite you with a ticket when you are caught speeding.

A CO (in reality) can be inmate's friend whether he is recognized as one or not. This officer is responsible for your safety, health and welfare. He is responsible for seeing to it that your meals are served on time. He is responsible for knowing your location at any given time and getting your mail delivered. When anything occurs in a prison out of the ordinary, the CO must be able to account for the event or activity and report it.

The correctional officers often work 30 hours overtime a week. That amounts to 70-hour workweeks. CO's may receive overtime pay but are usually given compensatory time, and most correctional facilities are understaffed daily. Many officers are forced to take days off because of work related stress and fatigue. Many employees, serving as adult and juvenile CO's are required to work extended hours. I believe the duties and responsibilities of these officers are often greater than sheriff's deputies, and local police officers. Yet their salaries are not equal. Sheriff's deputies and police offices usually command a larger salary

I believe it is important for inmates develop more respect for correctional officers and try understanding their mission. It is also important for CO's to develop more respect for inmates. Correctional officers are serving a population of convicted felons, including some who have serious mental and emotional problems. Some inmates have been convicted of crimes that are so shameful and heinous; they are too ashamed and frightened to acknowledge them. These officers are servicing a population that has demonstrated its willingness to violate criminal laws. They have committed acts of violence such as, home invasions, car hijackings, damage and theft of property, injuring and killing others with weapons, selling drugs, committing robberies, kidnappings, rape, burglaries and other acts of intimidation.

CO's, are sometimes verbally abused and physically assaulted by some inmates they are required to service. Remember our prison populations are composed of an extraordinarily large number of people who have mental illnesses, and emotional challenges. (One of five inmates has mental illnesses or emotional problems.) They do not necessarily respond to reasonable requests or orders presented by correctional officers. Correctional officers dealing with inmates who are unreasonable often find themselves working under very stressful conditions.

So please Mr. and Mrs. Inmate do not develop an attitude because the correctional officer or the guard does not trust you or he did not say please upon giving you an order. Why should he take your word, when he is serving a population that has violated the public trust. In reality, CO's realize they are dealing with people who have lied, stole and cheated others out of their property. Once a person is found guilty of violating the trust of someone, that person has to earn the trust of others.

A CO should be penalized, for taking the word of an inmate without verification. Trusted inmates usually carry the title of trustee. This title, and privileges that go with it must be earned.

Neither prison administrators nor their staff is responsible for an inmate's conviction and incarceration. Inmates benefit themselves when they understand relationships and demonstrate respect for those in authority over them.

We are created by God to be respected. When you respect yourself, you will be able to respect others. We are not talking about love. There is a big difference between respect and love. We respect the ocean because of its vastness, power, and depth. We do not necessarily love it. We have reasonable respect for a lion. Especially if it is free in its natural habitat, but we don't love it. When you cultivate enough respect for yourself and others, love may begin to germinate.

CHAPTER 12
MORALS AND MANNERS

I said earlier that I was born in Memphis, Tennessee and I lived there until nine years of age. It was during this time that I remember my mother teaching me to have good manners, morals, and be a "good boy." My mother taught me that I should "tip" my hat to a woman when passing her on the street. In addition, I was taught to open and hold doors for woman or girls before entering myself. She emphasized that these were acts of good manners. My mother was really teaching us the ways of Gods Prophets They were all mannerly men of good moral character. They were not boastful or rude. They were all modest in dress and deportment.

My mother began taking us to church as soon as we were all able to walk. Before taking us, she would give each child some coins to place in the offering plate. She taught us that giving in charity was our duty. While attending church we, were taught to tell the truth and be mindful of our behavior. We learned the 10 Commandments revealed to Moses before we were five years of age.

My mother instilled in me at a very early age that I should respect children and adults. This is not to say that I was the perfect child and never caused any difficulties. While a little boy I could be somewhat devilish. I would do things that were contrary to what my parents taught me. However, I am still conscious today of these lessons learned as a child. Over the years, I have learned that practicing good morals and manners helped me overcome various social challenges with minimum difficulties.

While studying the life of Prophet Muhammad, I learned he had great respect for motherhood. When asked by one of his companions, who was his best friend? He answered my mother. He was asked the second time. Who is your best friend? He answered again my Mother!! Prophet Muhammad (peace be upon him) then said the best friend after my mother is my father.

Every child should have a mother or a mother figure to teach it morals and manners. It is going to take morally strong mothers with good manners to reduce the number of young men and women that are going to prison. Islam demands of its adherents that they be sincere God-fearing and respectful. It demands of believers strong morality, sound sensitive human behavior and respect for everything in God's (Allah's') creation.

Morality is not a topic of which we can remain in different. It is the composite of the principles of life. All religions should adopt, care for, and respect the vehicle (Your Prophets) of its standard bearers. Your prophets were God-fearing men. They were respectable, virtuous and decent. If we collect all of the sayings of the holy Prophet about the importance of good moral character, we could prepare a voluminous book. Some people once asked the prophet "amongst the slaves of Allaah, Who Is the Dearest to Him? The Prophet replied "the one who has the best moral character." Prophet Muhammad (pbuh) once said "on the day of the judgment there will be nothing weightier in the balance of the Muslim then the goodness of his character."

He (Prophet Muhammad) was the best example of good moral character. Before he advised followers to adopt a strong moral life by giving sermons and counsel, he was sowing the seeds of morality by living an exemplary life.

All men and women (including inmates) have an obligation before Allah to be kind and decent toward their fellow men and women. We should not slander each other or backbite. We should help the weak and any others who are less fortunate than others in our society. If we do not feel the pain and suffering of others, we are not ready to join the universal community of men and women. Islam demands that its adherents remain conscious of the suffering of others and do what is reasonable to correct it.

I believe we are now living in Satan's world (The Devils world); a world of materialism. In this world, material things are valued more than human beings. For example, our society is so morally weak it often spends more money on health care for animals than people.

CHAPTER 13
ISLAM AND ITS POWER OF THE REDEMPTION

"Your Rights must end where another's rights begin." The United States Constitution states the following. "We hold these truths to be self evident, that all men are created equal, and they are endowed by their Creator (God) with certain inalienable rights. And, among these are life, liberty and the pursuit of happiness, and to secure these rights, governments are instituted among men, deriving their just powers from the consent of the governed." At the time the United States Constitution was accepted and approved, it did not apply to African slaves, ex-slaves or women in America. The United States Constitution has, since been amended, to include everyone regardless of race or sex. The Quran (the holy book of Muslims) states that God created every human being in the best mold; created him honorably and breathed something of His Spirit in him/her. The Muslim accepts the rights granted him by God through Quranic revelation. The rights granted citizens through the United States Constitution simply reinforce those rights granted by God (Allah). The Quran (a capitulation of the Bible, Torah and Injil), was revealed to Prophet Muhammad (pbuh) the last Messenger of God in Arabia over 1400 years ago. This book represents a design or pattern of life for all human beings. And Prophet Muhammad's life as he lived it, is regarded as the model or pattern for human behavior. His complete life is a living illustration of how we, as human beings, are supposed to live and conduct ourselves in relationship to God, and our fellow men

I believe men must be governed by something more powerful than themselves, if they are to exercise self control. "If a person is more powerful than another because of his/her strength, wealth or influence; and lacks respect for his fellow man, what prevents him/her from oppressing the weaker one? What prevents him from taking the weaker person's property or killing him and becoming a tyrant or dictator?

The law of the jungle does not apply in human behavior ("the survival of the fittest"). The survival of the biggest or the toughest, relative to human beings, is not a part Allah's law. Under God's law the strong must support and protect the weak.

I do not believe a man can control himself, unless he possesses an intelligent fear of displeasing (GOD) Allah. He has to believe that Allah Is in Control of His Creation and That He and He a Lone Is its Guardian, Evolver of all the worlds'. If one is not striving to please God, he finds himself striving to please the Devil. You cannot have it both ways. (You can't serve two masters.)

In America or any country, adults are expected to be self governed. Ours is a Democracy, a government of the people for the people and by the people." In a democracy there is no one standing over you to see if you are obeying the law. A democracy gives you the limited free will. God gave the human being limited free will when he was created. Men structured and patterned most of their laws, after Gods' prophetic law.

Our laws allow its citizens the freedom to do anything they want except disobey the law. In other words, it is OK to break the law, as long a you are not prosecuted. This is not a correct interpretation of freedom in a democracy. Freedom also represents a free mind. Your head is sometimes, described as a "dome". Hopefully, it is free.

Our democracy is a form of government established by the founding citizens of this country. Freedom and democracy defined in America's Constitution does not give its citizens the right to do anything they feel like doing. Freedom in our democracy means you have the right or the freedom to think for yourself and act accordingly. However, when you do not think for yourself, and act contrary to the law you can rest assured someone will think for you.

We said earlier, laws do not force you to "do the right thing." Laws are made for people who think for themselves and have the sensibility to respect the rights of others. Laws and guidelines are established to ensure a certain degree of order and promote justice. Regardless of our social or political status, we must all submit to the laws of our country in spirit and deed, if there is to be justice and freedom for all. For people to be able to live in a relatively peaceful society, they must agree to follow the guidelines of society.

Most people under the threat of sanctions will follow laws created by men. Yet, they cannot always be trusted to follow the law. They must be watched. You must have good traffic cops. This is interesting because many people profess to be God fearing and accept to follow the laws of God. Others do not accept that there is a God and fear the police more than they fear God. With a choice, I would rather live around people who are governed by an intelligent fear of God rather than live with people governed only by the police.

We need police officers however, people should be able to regulate themselves without fear of police officers overseeing them.

Those who identify themselves as Muslims have consciously accepted the reality that there is no God but one God and that Muhammad is God's last messenger. Persons declaring themselves Muslims are supposed to live for God's pleasure. Islam demands that human beings live decent lives. It demands that your behavior reflect a person of high moral character who strives to become a refined human being.

It demands that you help weak, sick, uneducated and oppressed people. Islam commands you help the immoral person as well as the morally strong. "You must want for your brother/sister that which you want for yourself". You must be a just person you must demand that justice be done even if it's against you or your loved ones. This is Allah's way.

Allah's Last Messenger was in no way a coward. Remember he was ordered by God to deliver the message of Islam while in a very hostile environment. How can a believer be cowardly? Cowardice is inconsistent with the behavior of one who fears Allah. Prophet Muhammad was born in Arabia approximately 570 A.D. His father Abdullah never had an opportunity to see his son because he became ill in Medina and died before the baby Muhammad was born. He was five years of age when his mother Ameenah became ill and died. Before he was six Muhammad the child was completely orphaned.

The period of time Prophet Muhammad was born and lived was called Al Jaahiliya or "the age of Ignorance." Warring tribes populated the peninsula of Arabia during this time and each tribe cherished its autonomy. (its individual freedom) Just as Prophet Muhammad was faced with warring tribes over 1400 years ago, we are faced with warring tribes today. During Muhammad's life, tribes would go to war with each other for trivial reasons. These tribes would have blood feud's. "An eye for an eye and a tooth for a tooth." These feuds could begin if one member of a tribe insulted a member from an opposite tribe. Differing tribal members had only to jostle another, or speak in an insulting tone or if an animal from another tribe drank from the "wrong well". Members of opposing tribes would begin fighting and killing each other and these feuds may go on for years. Warring tribes often would have long forgotten the cause of the fighting. Yet the fighting would continue because of foolish pride, arrogance and ignorance. (This scenario sounds familiar especially if you are a gang member or know something about gang behavior.

Most gang members today cannot offer logical reasons for their hatred towards each other. They often kill or maim each other with little if any provocation. They often kill or maim family members of gang associates.

We have other warring tribes in American society. They call themselves Democrats and Republicans; Liberals or Moderates; Conservatives, Feminist; Antiabortionist and pro-abortionist; Black and White Power Groups; the National Rifleman's Association etc. We have previously mentioned warring Tribes in our prison system. We Have the Bloods, Crips, Disciples, White Aryans, Skinheads and Rangers etc.

Just as the message of Islam brought about profound changes in the hearts and lives of the people of Arabia 1400 years ago, it can/will do the same in America today. In the beginning, most of the people of Mecca ignored Prophet Muhammad (PBUH) and refused to accept him as being Allah's last messenger. This made him feel very sad and he grieved for the people because of their ignorance. Before receiving Allah's message Muhammad was one of the most trusted men in the city of Mecca. He was referred to, as Al Amin "the trustworthy one." However, when Muhammad said he was the last messenger of God, he was no longer accepted by persons who had previously befriended him. Some said, he was beguiled by a witch, or had lost his mind. He challenged the people by stating, "If I told you that there was an Army on the other side of that mountain and that this army was going to attack you, would you believe me?" They said, yes we would believe you Al Amin, because you have never lied to us before.

Almighty God, Allah begin revealing His Message To Prophet Muhammad at the age of 40 and it was revealed by the Angel Jabril. (Gabriel) Prior to receiving revelation, Muhammad would spend many hours alone seeking solitude, by retreating to a cave on Mount Nur (the Mountain of light). He would go to this cave and remain for extended lengths of time while meditating and reflecting on his relationship to Allah. In addition, he lamented over social and spiritual conditions of the people with whom he lived. He was constantly attempting to reconcile the oppressive and immoral life styles of the people.

During this time, in Arabia, physical and social living conditions were harsh. (The desert environment can evoke a dual emotional response.) It can promote compassionate or selfish hardheartedness.) Prophet Muhammad delivered a message of hope for 10 years in this environment, in Mecca, and its countryside. The message was simple. "There is no

God but Allah and I am The Messenger of God." Soon tribal leaders gathered and plotted to prevent Prophet Muhammad from delivering this message.

Prophet Muhammad's uncle, Abu Talib, who served as Muhammad's guardian after the death of his parents, warned him about the plot. His uncle also told Muhammad that Arabia's leaders offered him gifts of great wealth such as, women, live stock and gold provided he stop teaching the message of the oneness of Allah and that he was the Messenger of Allah. They also promised to make him their leader. He reflected these offers and afterwards told his uncle "if they could place the Sun in my right hand and the moon in my left I would not stop preaching the message of Allah."

After ten years and avoiding an assassination attempt Prophet Muhammad was ordered by Allah, to migrate to Medinah. He was driven out of Mecca by the tribes of Arabia because they opposed the message of Islam. Muhammad taught, man was not to worship anything of this creation nor was he to associate anything with God. He taught that neither man, his tribal or nationalistic ties were as important as his relationship to God. Those who accepted this message, and worshipped God without any associates, found that they had the strength to ignore their tribal relationships when necessary while seeking unity among men in the cause of Allah.

Prophet Muhammad is the only Prophet in history whose life is historically documented from his birth to time of his death. The Message of Muhammad, (the Quran) radically changed the hearts and minds of all persons of faith. Those who believed the message and had not doubts or reservations about it soon became staunch converts, supporters, and followers of Allah's last Messenger

"This Is the Book; in it is guidance sure, without doubt for those who fear Allah; who believe in the unseen, who are steadfast in prayer and spend out of what We have provided for them; and who believe in the revelation sent before their time; in their hearts have the assurance of the hereafter. Those who are on true guidance from their Lord, it is these who will prosper." (Qur'an chapter 2 verses 2-5). "

Everyone, including inmates should study the life of Prophet Muhammad and seek to pattern their lives after him. The writer makes this assertion, in an effort to assist inmates serving time with minimal difficulty. The Quran teaches that Allah is often for giving and He Is Most Merciful. Allah hears every prayer and He Is As Close to You and your jugular vein. He is your Creator and your protector. This chapter is a brief summary of the life of Prophet Muhammad and the Quran.

I encourage everyone to do their own research, and study the Quran and the life of Prophet Muhammad. Allah desires that each of His servants received their personal revelation by studying Quran for themselves. Inmates are encouraged to get to know themselves and learn to be themselves. "Your self is a righteous Muslim".

Allah revealed the following to Muhammad. "You are my Prophet and my slave servant. The people are also my slaves. Oh! Muhammad you are to deliver the message! You are not here to oversee the people. They Will Accept My Message from you or they will reject it. You are not responsible for them except to deliver my message." Allah revealed to Prophet Muhammad that He will determine whether or not His slaves receive His Message. (Man does not have the capacity to save himself or anyone else.) "He will never change the condition of a people until they change what is troubling their hearts." If your heart is corrupt and you are entertaining diabolical plots against your fellow human being, why should Allah bless you to see or hear anything? It is your individual obligation as a human being to decide for yourself to study God's Word. To have faith in God is a personal commitment that one has to make for him/herself. How can you believe in yourself without first believing in God? God created you Muslim. It is now up to you to accept that you are Muslim. Remember the word Muslim describes anything or anybody that submits to Allah. You were created, to serve God. You had no choice in the matter. God said, "Be" and here you are.

CHAPTER 14
THE FIVE PILLARS (ARTICLES) OF FAITH IN ISLAM

Prophet Muhammad (PBUH) taught that Islam, the submission or surrender to God, is supported by five articles or pillars of faith. To understand this concept of five pillars use the construction or the design of a simple tent. A tent has a taller center pole with four slightly shorter poles at each corner. We can visualize how these five pillars support the structure of the tent. These principles or five pillars represents goals, standards or duties of man. And, according to God's plan the pillars symbolize the character of Islamic society.

(I). The first pillar (represented by the center pole) is the belief in the oneness of God and the belief that Prophet Muhammad of Arabia, born over 1400 years ago is Allahs' Last Messenger. This first article of faith also represents the Declaration each believer makes once he/she accepts the reality of the oneness of Allah. The person accepting the reality of the oneness of God becomes a witness (Shaheed). Each believer must make their personal declaration affirming the oneness of Allah and that Muhammad is His Messenger and he/she accepts to be a Muslim (an obedient servant of Allah). One can only be a witness when they have seen and realized the object of their testimony.

An informed person with faith in God, can come to the realization that there is only one God and Prophet Muhammad is his Messenger. It is one's faith that determines whether Allah will allow him/her to grasp the significance of the oneness of God.

We are only allowed to see, hear and understand through God's volition. ("God never changes the condition of a people until they change what is troubling their hearts.")

(II.) The Second Pillow of Faith Is Prayer. Everyone who declares themselves Muslim is obliged pray five times daily at prescribed times, This is the way of Prophet Muhammad. Allah ordained prayer through the examples Of His last Messenger.

(1.) The first prayer is the morning prayer (Fajir). This prayer is recited immediately after dawn and before sunrise. This prayer consists of two rakahs'.

(2.) The second prayer (noon day prayer) (Zhur) is recited immediately after the sun passes its Zenith. This prayer consists of four (rakahs').

(3.) The third prayer (midday prayer)(Asr) is recited during the middle of the day and it consists of four (Rakas')

(4.) The fourth prayer (sunset prayer)(Mahgrib) is recited immediately after sunset and this prayer consists of three (Rakas).

(5.) The fifth prayer, the night prayer (Ishaa) or evening prayer is recited before retiring at the end of the day. This prayer consists of four (rakas).

Prayer in Islam is an obligation on every able-bodied believer. There are some exceptions that one learns through practice and study. Prayer is an integral part of one's life in Islam and when ever it is possible, believers are encouraged to come together and pray in a group.

Muslims are encouraged to pray together daily if possible. However, it is obligatory that they come together for group prayer every Friday. Friday prayer is called (jumah prayer). The Arabic word for prayer is (Salat). Every Friday Muslims are obligated to pray Salatul Jumah. Friday is the Muslims day of group worship.

III. The third pillar of faith is charity, or (Zakat). Believers must be charitable. Giving donations and supporting those in need is a duty that must be fulfilled. The Muslim must seek out those in need and help them. The believer does not wait for the needy to come to him as a beggar. Your duty is to find the needy before they have to resort to begging. If you do not have money to give or property, you can give a smile or a helping hand whenever possible. Zakat or charity is an organized institution in Islam. The believer is required to donate a certain portion of his/her capital worth annually. Public welfare (charity) was designed by God, and implemented by His messengers. The poor has a right to a share of your wealth and it is the Muslims duty to implement Zakat as a means towards this end. Islam introduced nationally organized welfare for the good of those who were less fortunate (the weak and the helpless) over 1400 years ago.

(IV) The fourth pillar of Faith is fasting during the month of Ramadan. Ramadan is the ninth month in the lunar year. During this time the Muslim must deny him/herself food and drink during the daylight hours. This fast will last for a maximum of 29 days. The fast begins with the sighting of the new moon which signals the beginning of the month of Ramadan. The fast continues until the sighting of the next new moon. Fasting Muslims must break the fast immediately after sunset each day by eating a few dates and drinking water or perhaps fruit juice. After praying Mahgrib (after sunset), the Muslim may eat his/her meal for the day. This meal should be modest and believers are to avoid gluttony.

(V)The Fifth Pillar of faith is the Hajj or the pilgrimage. Every adult Muslim who enjoys good health and have the financial means to do so, must make the Hajj at least once during their life. The Hajj is called many things including "the journey of a lifetime." The Hajj (which means struggle) symbolizes the completion of one's faith. The pilgrimage also represents ones participation in the global convention of human beings.

Muslims have six fundamental beliefs. These include the five pillars or principles of Islam. Muslims believe in the oneness of Allah (God). Muslims believe in all of God's Prophet's from Adam to Muhammad. Muslims do not deny or question the existence of any of Gods' Prophet's. Muslims believe in God's books And His Angels. They believe in the day of resurrection (the Day of judgment, reward and punishment) Muslims believe in Allah's Divine ordinance; the belief that all power proceeds from Allah.

Much can be said about the articles of faith and the principles of Islam. This book however is not designed nor has the capacity to encompass the unending aspects of the pillars and articles of faith. It is hoped that the reader will be encouraged to pursue his/her independent study of Islam.

"Say, we believe in Allah and what has been revealed to us and what was revealed to all of his Prophets, including Abraham, Ishmael, Isaac and the Tribes, And the Books revealed to Moses, Jesus and the Prophets from their Lord. We make no distinction between any one among them, and to Allah do we bow our Will in Islam". (Qur'an 3:84 The Family of Imran)

The more one studies Allah's revelation Through His Last Messenger, the more one realizes Islam promotes a unified balanced way of life. The main theme in Quran Is the Oneness of God.

CHAPTER 15

How Criminal Behavior Is Defined

Criminal Laws defined criminal behavior. Our laws are established by state legislators and these laws are passed for "the greater good of society." There are special interest groups, agencies and associations that work to influence members of Congress when civil or criminal laws are considered. There are professional lobbyist, hired by special interest groups, to promote certain laws and oppose others. Consequently, all laws passed are not necessarily passed for the greater good.

For example; there was a time when a few young men gathered on a street corner visiting and joking with each other was accepted forms of behavior. In the early 1950's through the early 60s young African-American male youths would gather on street corners and sing together in groups. Often these singing groups would compete with each other to see who could harmonize the best or who could perform the best dance routine as they sang. These youths, were attempting to emulate popular professional African-American singing groups such as the "Four Tops, The Orioles, The Ravens, the Temptations, The Spinners etc. etc. They would entertain themselves and pedestrians as they walked by. The young men were not intimidating and they were not vulgar. Many of them were excellent singers and entertainers.

Laws have since been passed in some states making it a crime if two or more young men gather on the public way. When two or more young men gather now they can be arrested, and possibly charged with gang conspiracy. Between 1950 and 1965 illicit drugs such as crack cocaine, "blunts", and date rape cocktails had not completely permeated many African-American communities. In the latter part of the 1960s marijuana was the drug of choice among many college and high school students regardless of race. In the early 1960s African-American youths began to change their patterns of behavior. Street gangs emerged in full force during this period 1965 through 1975 youth. This was the beginning of violent ongoing "turf" battles.

The level of violence was only limited at this time because semiautomatic weapons and rifles were not as readily available to street gangs as they are today. This is not to suggest that these warring gangs or tribes were not "hell-bent" on destroying each other. They had the will, but their ability to kill and maim was limited. They lacked the resources.

Today thanks to the National Rifle Association, arms manufacturers, and others, automatic weapons and semiautomatic weapons are available to anyone seeking them. Gang violence today has escalated exponentially because of wars between gangs to control and regulate an increasingly lucrative drug trade. The wars to control drug trafficking in our large cities and in some of our small cities have spread like prairie fires across the country.

Today no community is safe to from the possibility of an instant act of murderous violence due to a drug deal gone sour. Because of this level of violence and increasing drug use, laws' governing illicit drugs and court sentencing have changed. Not only have laws changed, they are constantly being monitored. Public school systems have demanded and obtained changes in laws governing students. (For example. search and seizure's on school property and a students property considered to be contraband.)

Public schools can no longer function without legally addressing very real problems of drugs and gang violence. Laws have been implemented allowing schoolchildren to be searched while using drug sniffing dogs to search their lockers. Metal detectors are now used in many major public-school systems.

The problem of illicit drug use in America has grown so much that our society has changed its rules of engagement. 50 years ago, if you were under the influence of narcotics such as heroin or cocaine, you could have been arrested and charged with being a loitering addict. At that time, if you were thought to be under the influence of drugs you were subject to arrest and prosecution. Today it is no longer a crime to be addicted to illicit drugs. An addict today is considered a drug abuser in need of treatment.

Treatment for drug addiction has been around since the introduction of alcohol in America. Drug abuse treatment (itself) maybe looked upon as a new discipline. This is a misnomer. Because of the need to address the accelerating proliferation of drug abuse in the workplace and in general populations, laws guidelines, workplace rules, regulations etc. have to be changed and new ones introduced.

Many corporate executives are addicted to illicit drugs. They too are in drug treatment programs. If companies fired every corporate executive that was addicted to drugs the companies production would suffer unacceptable loses .

In America the problem of drug abuse is so pervasive that it is increasingly difficult to recruit and maintain a drug free workforce. The criminal justice system has a serious drug abuse problem within its workforce. And so does every United States branch of our military. Drug addiction, has no social, financial, or educational boundaries. America now has an over abundance of drug addicted doctors, lawyers, policeman, correctional officers, nurses, social workers, psychiatrist, psychologist and others.

The American public consumes over 70% of all illicit drugs produced by foreign countries. And our prison population explosion can be directly attributed to the illegal use and sale of drugs. America's war on drugs was lost long before it began. America's craving for illicit drugs will determine if it can win or lose its war on drugs. Foreign drug cartels will always find ways to produce and ship drugs into America as long as the demand is there. Most drug producing countries are financing many of their government programs with money that is raised from marketing their drugs to U.S. citizens.

Wealth and power was corrupting governments long before American came into existence. Our government's credibility has been lost in the eyes of other governments that are producing illicit drugs. We are viewed as being hypocritical in our attempt to present moral arguments against countries that are marketing "illicit drugs" in America. Illicit drug trafficking, local and international price-fixing, and amoral trade relationships with other countries has undermined out governments moral strength and credibility. We cannot effectively pursue our mismanaged war on drugs because our government is not trusted to do the right thing.

This writer recalls in the 1950s when illicit drugs were not considered to be a serious problem. However, illicit drugs was a serious social, moral and economically debilitating problem in many African-American communities. Illicit drug use was not "affecting" America's white communities. Now "the genie is out of the bottle". Many inmates in prison today are there because of crimes related to or influenced by drugs.

CHAPTER 16

"ISLAM IS NOT A BLACK RELIGION"

Islam, its philosophy, and way of life is stigmatized negatively by America's media. Its adherents are identified as terrorists and Islam is said too be a religion that promotes terrorism. In addition, Islam is identified with Black Nationalism or "Black Power organizations". These misconceptions promote divisiveness and incite racists' views pitting whites against blacks. These false ideas have caused some Americans to think that Islam is an exclusive Black man's religion. Islam, has also been identified as a religion attractive only to African-Americans who perhaps are mentally challenged.

However, after the collapse of the Union of the Soviet Socialist Republic (the Russian government), many political thinkers and US government lawmakers predicted that the next greatest challenge to America and its way of life would be

Islam. These thinkers knew that Russia's government collapsed because its war with the Islamic nation of Afghanistan.

The image of Islam being a racist and anti-American religion grew out of the effects of Caucasian racism. In the early 1940s a gentleman by the name of Elijah (Poole) Muhammad began to address the African-American community concerning racism in America. It was Muhammad's disgust with how African-Americans were mistreated, that prompted the establishment of the Nation of Islam. Elijah Muhammad, through his tireless teachings and faith in Allah, established a religious community of exclusively African Americans. This tightly knit organization of African Americans, identified as the "Nation of Islam suddenly exploded on the American scene between 1950 and 1960. This community of Muslims became internationally known as the "Nation of Islam" and its members became known as Black Muslims.

Malcolm Malik Shabazz, who was popularly referred to as Brother Malcolm, also known as Malcolm X, joined the Nation of Islam in the early 50s. It was through Malcolm's faith in God, his dedication to the Nation of Islam, his fiery speeches and demonstrated courage that helped thrust the Nation of Islam into the forefront of American politics and civil rights movement. Brother Malcolm did not back down nor did he compromise in his condemnation of racism in America.

This courageous man was assassinated under, unusual circumstances on February 21, 1965. Prior to Malcolm's assassination, he was in the process of preparing a case to present to the United Nations. This brave man was going to condemn America before the Worlds Public (United Nations)for its continued perpetration of a litany of injustices committed against African-American citizens . In the eyes of those who opposed Justice for all in America, this action was dreaded. In their eyes, this condemnation of America for its treatment of its African-American citizens would have been too politically embarrassing. Its difficult to condemn other countries of suppressing human rights and democracy, when you are guilty of the same practices.

Elijah Muhammad, whom we once referred to as the Honorable Elijah Muhammad had publicly condemned Brother Malcolm for a comment that he had made regarding the assassination of President John F. Kennedy. This condemnation, along with government provocateurs, jealousy, arrogance, and fear led to Malcolm's assassination.

10 years after the assassination of Brother Malcolm, in 1975 the Honorable Elijah Muhammad died in a Chicago hospital after a prolonged illness.

Elijah Muhammad's son Wallace Deen Muhammad was elected to succeed his father as the head of the nation of Islam in 1975.

Wallace D. Muhammad began to teach the religion of Islam, according to the Quran and the Sunnah of Prophet Muhammad. Wallace D. Muhammad now referred as Imam Warith Uddin Muhammad is currently the respected leader of the largest number of Muslims in America. He is internationally known and respected by many learned scholars of Islam. Since 1975, he has tirelessly presented the philosophy of Islam to audiences in America and numerous other countries.

In 1979 a gentleman, known as, Minister Louis Farrakhan, a former Minister and disciple of Elijah Muhammad, began teaching the old philosophy of his mentor. Minister Farrakhan began teaching the old philosophy of the late Honorable Elijah Muhammad. He too is a sincere, dedicated, and eloquent Islamic leader. He continues to express legitimate concerns about social conditions in the African-American community of America. This was the way of the Honorable Elijah Muhammad.

Minister Farrakhan would "roast" racists Caucasian's at every opportunity. He was an apt pupil of Elijah Muhammad. With his condemnation of racism and injustices home and abroad, Minister Farrakhan has been a constant embarrassment for America's public and its government. During this period Mr. Farrakhan would encourage his followers to establish their own community and to seek a physical separation from Caucasians.

In February 2000, members of the Nation of Islam and followers of the Imam WarithUddin Muhammad jointly attended a meeting in Chicago. This holiday (Holy Day) is called "Saviors Day". I do not profess to know the significance of this joint meeting and celebration. However, Minister Louis Farrakhan and Imam Muhammad did greet and embrace each other.

The history of the Honorable Elijah Muhammad, ImamWarithuddin Muhammad, Malcolm Malik Shabazz, Muhammad Ali, (The first Muslim Worlds Heavy Weight Champion) strongly suggests, it was these men who helped popularize Islam in America.

In 1913, before Elijah Muhammad begin cultivating an interest in Islam, an African American by the name of a Noble Drew Ali began to encourage African-Americans to look to Africa (The country of Morocco) for their physical, social, educational and religious salvation. Ali saw a connection between the Islamic country of Morocco and the former Black slaves of America.

He has followers today that identify themselves as Muslims. Noble Drew Ali was the founder of the Moorish Science Temple of America and he established the first Temple in Newark, New Jersey. In 1913, he published a book referred to as "The "Holy Koran" of the Moorish holy Temple of science. (This is not the Quran revealed to Prophet Muhammad over 1400 years ago.) This local Newark organization grew into a national institution that included temples in major American cities.

Noble Drew Ali advocated that African-Americans should drop the identity As Blacks and Negroes and see themselves as members of the African nation of Morocco. In 1929 Noble Drew Ali was arrested and charged with the murder of one of his associates. Though the charges were questionable, Noble Drew Ali never went to trial. Allegedly, he was beat to death by other inmates (murdered) while in jail.

His fate was similar to that of many African-Americans who had the audacity to challenge racism and injustice in America. The Moorish science Temple of America has many followers today they refer to themselves as Moorish Americans, and many study the "Koran" that was written by Noble Drew Ali.

Since we are on the subject of Morocco, I think it would be a good idea to look briefly at its history and relationship to our country (U.S.A.) The message of Islam became the major social influence in North Africa in about 700 A.D. In approximately 750 A.D., the Islamic country Morocco received and accepted an invitation from Spain to enter its country and support it against German tribes and others who were terrorizing its countryside.

After driving out the German invaders' Muslim Moroccans established a just Islamic society in Spain that lasted for over 700 years. During this period, Spain had paved roads, public baths, lighted streets, and running water.

This advanced European country of Spain, under the influence of Islam launched the renaissance. Historians often over look the reality that it was Islam and its redeeming precepts and practices that rescued Europe through Spain from "The Dark Ages". None questioned the authority of Kings or Churches in Europe until the introduction of Islam. During the "Dark Ages" kings, and leaders of churches were worshipped by their subjects. (The people) whom they ruled with an iron hand

Marcus Garvey is another great African American historical figure. He challenged Americas' acts of racism and social injustice. Marcus was born in Jamaica and travel to America in 1917. He is the founder of The Universal Negro Improvement Association (UNIA). This became the largest organization in the history of America dedicated to black economic independence, self-determination and racial pride. The (UNIA) under Garvey's leadership created chapters through out the U.S., Central and South America, the West Indies, West Africa, England and Canada. The (U.N.I.A.) created The Negro Factories Corp in 1918. This association supported the national development of black businesses. In 1918, a doll factory was developed that produced doll's and hired over 1000 workers. One of Garvey's greatest accomplishments was the creation of the Black Steamship Line. This was an enterprise to provide a way for African-Americans to return to Africa. It would also allow them to exchange goods and services around the Atlantic Ocean. This company owned three ocean going ships. One of them named the S.S. Frederick Douglas. Ownership of the Black Star Line made trade and travel possible between the United States the Caribbean, Central and South America and many African countries.

Garvey's visionary efforts to strengthen the steamship line met with furious opposition from competing national business, racism and duplicitous African-Americans. (African dupes were also labeled Boot lickers, Uncle Toms or Handkerchief heads").

In 1922 Garvey was indicted by the United States government and charged with mail fraud. He was convicted and received a maximum sentence of five years imprisonment by judge Julian Mack, a staunch member of the NAACP. (The National Association for the advancement Of Colored People.) "One has to wonder how the NAACP was advancing the cause of colored people by persecuting a prominent and successful leader like Marcus Garvey? He entered a federal penitentiary in Atlanta, Georgia but his followers began a petition drive protesting his illegal conviction. They demanded and obtained his release, after protesting for nearly 3 years. When Garvey was released in 1925, he was deported to Jamaica. He was legally barred from ever returning to America.

While in Jamaica, he continued his worldwide struggle for social justice and economic independence for black people. Garvey died in 1940 after suffering from a second stroke. Historians agree that the Jamaican Rastafarian movement, and the Nation of Islam were heavily influenced by the United Negro Improvement Association and the Moorish American Organization. Many members of these organizations soon joined the Nation of Islam.

The author mentioned the above historical personalities to help the reader gain some understanding and appreciation for these great African-Americans. Their struggles are identified with the history of today's African American Muslim community. These leaders past and present have significantly influenced the evolution that is occurring within the Islamic psyche of African American communities and the American Islamic community.

Before America came into existence, the influence of Islam had brought many African nations to the zenith of their social, economical, educational and moral development. Great Islamic centers of education including the first known University were established in African nations. We have briefly summarized some Islamic history of the country Morocco. However, we neglected to mention that Morocco was the first nation to recognize America as an independent country. Morocco extended this recognition to America, before Britain accepted her independence. During this period, Britain was the colonial power of North America.

I have observed Muslims of foreign countries, who have strong disagreements with our country's government and its policies. I have watched immigrant Muslims seek to influence the thinking of African-American Muslims. My purpose for making these observations is to help keep those who are seriously considering the religion of Islam from becoming confused by "False Prophets".

Racism has no place in Islam. If You a Looking for a Black Or White religion, you will not find it in Islam. Racism is very much like a skunk. For Example the skunk is clearly marked with black and white fur. There is no question about its identity. When a skunk becomes agitated or fearful, it sprays a foul smelling liquid from the rear of its body. If you have ever had a confrontation with a polecat, a skunk that has discharged its scent, you know exactly what I'm talking about. You will have a Foul-Smelling situation.

When a person or an institution makes decisions based solely on race it does not smell right. How can one make a fair and just decision when the decision-making process is driven by the color of one's skin or nationality? This behavior will stink up the place.

When Prophet Muhammad made his last address during his final Haji in Mecca, he spoke to many social issues including those of justice, fairness and racism. "This day I have perfected your religion for you and completed my favor unto you, and have chosen for you as a religion, Islam (Quran 5.3)

THE LAST SERMON OF PROPHET MUHAMMAD
"I bear witness that there is no God but one God, the one having no partner with him. He fulfilled his promise and granted victory To His bondsman, And He Alone defeated

the Confederates (the enemies of Islam.) People, listen to my words, for I do not know whether we shall ever meet again and perform Hajj, after this year. Oh people, Allah said we have created you from one male and one female and made you into tribes and nations, that you may know one another. Surely, in the sight of Allah, the most honored among you is, the one who is most God-fearing. There is no superiority of an Arab over a none Arab and for a non-Arab over an Arab, nor for a white over a black or for a black over a white except by piety and good action.

People, verily the lands, the property and the honor of each person is sacred and inviolable until you appear before Allah, as the sacred inviolability of this day, this month and in this town. Verily you will soon meet Allah and you will be held answerable for your actions.

Oh people; fear Allah concerning women. And, surely you have your rights over your wives and they have theirs over you. Behold! It is not permissible for a woman to give anything from the wealth of her husband to anyone but with his consent.

Beware no one else is responsible for a crime other than the one who commits it.

Behold! All practices of the days of ignorance are now under my feet. The blood revenges of the days of ignorance are now voided. All interests and usurious (interest charges) during and from the times of ignorance are abolished.

Oh People, every Muslim is a brother to every other Muslim and all the Muslims form one brotherhood.

Take heed not to go astray after me, and kill one another.

He who (amongst you) has anything placed in trust with him, must return it to its owner.

Oh People, listen to and obey even a slave if he is your Amir (leader) and if he executes (the ordinances of) the Book among you.

VERILY, I have left amongst you that which if you follow, you will never go astray, the Book of Allah and the Tradition of His Messenger. Beware of committing excesses in the matters of religion, for it is excesses in religion, that brought destruction to (many people) before you.

VERILY, Satan has despaired of being worshipped in this land of yours, but if he can be obeyed in anything short of worship, he will be pleased: so beware of him in matters of your religion.

Muhammad then asked the pilgrims, "Have I conveyed (The message)?" They replied yes, you have conveyed the Message and fulfilled your mission." Then the Prophet said, O

Allah, be my witness." (The Sunnah of Prophet Muhammad) (P.B.H.U.)

The Message of Muhammad is not an exclusively directed message for any particular people, nation or race. This is Allah's message for all people for all times. It is not exclusive of any group. It is for all religions and for all people who worship Allah, whether intentional or unintentional. You have a right to read and study the Quran and you do not need any ones permission. I am writing in this manner because there are people who do not feel authorized to read the Quran or study Islam without special approval.

There are also "Muslims" who feel that you are not qualified to study or teach Islam unless you have a "chosen wise man" sponsor you, or grant his permission.. Remember Allah gave you intelligence the same as the "wise". God says, "He is as close to you as your jugular vein".

CHAPTER 17

IT IS OFFICIAL! YOU ARE NOW AN INMATE

Where do we go from here, now that you are in the "Big House"? (This is a state or federal prison.) It may have been a long time coming but you finally made it. Who knows, because of your life style or other circumstances, you may have been headed for prison since childhood. Perhaps some of your associates or relatives warned you that you were headed towards the Big House but you didn't listen.

Only Allah knows why you are in prison. Some may say you were sexually, mentally, and physically abused as a child and this is caused you to "act out" leading to your conviction. Maybe you came from a "broken home". (What is a broken home?) Some may say your home is broken if you do not have both parents living with you. Others say your home is broken if your mother is a "crack head" or a prostitute.

Maybe your family was poor and your parents were unable to purchase things described as childhood needs. Maybe you had both parents, a mother and father, but they were always "bugging" you or tripping". Maybe you just got sick and tired of people telling you what or what not to do. You just got sick of people meddling in your business. Only Allah knows. We can continue searching for reasons but we can do nothing about the pass. We have to deal with the present.

Perhaps you began your journey to prison as a juvenile because you were a African American or a "Latino". Yes, social circumstances and influences surrounding ones race, ethnicity or nationalistic ties can play a significant role towards programming a juvenile to enter prison. The writer clearly understands that racism can become a significant variable in determining whether or not a young person will or will not go to prison as a juvenile or an adult.

Because of systemic racism in America, an African American youth, man or women driving an automobile is more likely to be stopped by the police than a White motorist. All things being equal, it is usually the Black motorist who will be pulled over.

It has become a standing joke among some African Americans who often described their traffic victimization as follows. I was given a traffic summons because of D.W.B.

("Driving While Black".) Some mentally alert African Americans are familiar with a term in traffic enforcement called (DUI) "Driving Under the Influence of Alcohol. A (D.W.B.) Driving while black has become a de facto traffic violation for Black motorist.

If there are any doubts about the assertion of systemic racism in our country please refer to surveys and studies conducted relative to racism and traffic enforcement in America. Though African Americans represent 13-15% of this nations population, this group receives nearly 40% of all traffic tickets issued. A recent article written in the Arizona Republic newspaper in April 26, 2000 appeared under the headline of "Race Bias in Juvenile Justice." I will quote this article because for the sake of the many who still insist racial bias do not exists in law enforcement. This myopic view explains away the disparity by declaring that African Americans commit more crimes than others. This accounts for the larger numbers of Black arrestees compared to whites.

Black youths are six times more likely to be arrested and locked up than their white peers. This report was released by the Youth Law Center, and researched by the National Council on Crime and Delinquency. This report maintains that racial bias exist at every step in the juvenile justice system. "We know that there is racism in the system", said

Eleanor Eisenberg, executive director of the Arizona branch of the American Civil Liberties Union. "A White kid from a middle or upper income background is more apt to be given a warning and sent home. Minority youths are more likely than their whites counter parts to be arrested, held in jail, sent to trial, convicted and given longer prison sentences the report says. "It is astounding our nation can tolerate such gross inequality," said William Spriggs, director of research and public policy for the Urban League. "We cannot have a justice system that works this way."

We have discussed a number of things about racism and bias in the above paragraphs. However, the fact remains that you are now an inmate. You may be Caucasian, Hispanic, etc. You are still confined. Your house is now a 6 X 9 foot cell, and if you are lucky depending upon how you look at it, you maybe confined to 3'X 9' cubicle in a large dormitory setting.

You can no longer raid the refrigerator like you did at home while living with your parents. You are no longer free to go outside and take a walk when you feel like it.

You may or may not see or hear a bird in flight or hear one singing until you walk out of a particular prison. And, if you ever eat ice- cream while incarcerated, you will consider it a miracle. You can no longer personally speak to your mother or embrace her unless she visits you, and you still may not be able to embrace her. You may be confined in a prison that is 100 or more miles from your home. Your permanent place of residence is now the prison. Get used to it and do not fight it. (You must make adjustments while in prison.) You may not accept confinement but you must adjust to it. Your parents or other loved ones may or may not own an automobile. And, remember their car was not purchased for the sole purpose of visiting you while you are in prison.

It takes time and effort for family members to make prison visits, and a prison is not a pleasant place for to visit. Gasoline cost nearly $5.00 a gallon and your relatives may have to take a day off from work to pay you a visit.

You will have to make new friends in prison. You will see some of your old friends ("Hommys") as you call them). You were probably wondering what happened to them before you were convicted and sentenced. They had disappeared. Now you know why. They are in prison awaiting your arrival. You maybe assigned a bunk near an old friend. Some prisons staff attempt to accommodate inmates who are reasonable and not prone to be "trouble makers". Your prison's biggest challenge and concern is keeping peace within their walls. The last thing a warden needs is a serious conflict between inmates. The newly arrived inmate must first acclimate himself to his prison environment. If you have a problem with anger management, you had better start controlling you temper immediately. Remember, most of your prison associates have similar problems. If you have been previously diagnosed with any mental or emotional disorder such as A.D.H.D. (Attention Deficit Hyperactive Disorder), O.D.D.(Oppositional Defiant Disorder),or a Bi Polar, welcome to the club. You and your fellow inmates have been determined menaces to society, and one out of five prison inmates suffer mental or emotional disorders. In addition, some are under clinical medication.

Fear not, you can survive in this environment, and you can survive as a human being regardless of the nature of your crime. The choice is yours. Your imprisonment can serve as a blessing or a curse. That fact that you are still living suggests that your ultimate destiny is yet unfolding. Why are you still living and what is your purpose? These are questions and challenges that only you can purposely resolve and meet.

Reality awaits us all and there are no exceptions, and there are challenges that we must meet in our lives before we can recognize our purpose. One of the conditions of recognizing reality is accepting the existence of God. The many mysteries of our universe, affirm the reality of God. We exist because we exist and we cannot control its beginning or ending. This universe in which we live, was created by an indescribable intellectual force. Something designed and ordered our creation. "He is the Lord of all the worlds. No associate has He, of this I am commanded and I am of the first to submit."

When an inmate is blessed with the knowledge of the existence and Oneness of Allah (God), he has reached a significant turning point in his/her life. In addition, he/she is well on their way toward establishing a peacefully rewarding life for themselves and others.

I encourage inmates to "do your time" in the most peaceful manner possible. Do not look for trouble because trouble has found you. Your mission while in prison is to avoid trouble whenever possible. If you cannot avoid trouble, meet it head on. "Truth stands on its own and will always prevail but falsehood by its very nature must perish." Lies cannot endure. Try to be reasonably helpful to your fellow inmate when possible. Assist (COs) correctional officers or guards by following prison rules and regulations.

Do not be a "smart ass." Talk but do not talk too much. Feel good about yourself. God says in Quran, "He created you in the best mold and breathed something of His Spirit into you." Do not see yourself as a victim. Think for your self and do not allow anyone to think for you. Do not be a "snitch."

If anyone requests information from you about some else, refer questioner to the person that they are inquiring about. In other words, "don't ask me about anyone. If you want to know about someone, I suggest you go and ask that person yourself".

Do not carry your feelings on your shoulders. Everyone is not your enemy, nor is everyone wishing you "bad luck". Don't act paranoid. Voice your opinion only when its' requested. "Do not ask questions when if answered will be a problem for you", and do not attempt to change the opinion of another.

Remember, everyone has an opinion and everyone is entitled to voice an opinion. To suggest that one should not offer an opinion is to suggest that they do not have a mind or a brain of their own.

You are in prison for a reason. Make the most of it.

"Take advantage of five things before five others occur.

1.) Take advantage of your leisure before you get busy. 2.) Take advantage of your health before you get sick. 3.) Take advantage of your wealth before you become poor. 4.) Take advantage of your youth before you get old, and 5.) Take advantage of your life before you die."

CHAPTER 18
YOUR FAMILY

`Inmates have obligations to families they left, upon their incarceration. Some of my questions to inmates, concerning their families, are as follows; what do you think about those whom you left behind or do you ever think about them? How are they getting along without you? Do you think they miss you and would like to see you, or at least know that you are well?

Is your absence creating a hardship for your family? How are your children, and other relatives and friends? What about the welfare of other children that you and your "frequent flyer mile unlisted associates" may have produced? Many inmates before their incarceration glorified in having babies with as many different women as possible. Often young women will seek to become pregnant by their "hero dope peddler" friend because of a percieved unlimited source of income. If you were one of those dope peddlers or "pharmacist" before your incarceration, you understand what I am speaking of.

Think about the possibly unlisted babies and "girl friends" your arrest has left in the lurch. Inmates should soon begin communicating with their family, and friends. Write letters regularly. Write encouraging your children to get good grades in school and obey their parents and teachers.

Writing your children is significantly important and you should be honest with them. Children respect and love their parents regardless of their circumstances. Advise your children to live decent lives. Encourage them to always speak the truth and be honest. Admit your shortcomings to your children and tell them to guard against repeating your mistakes. People in their right minds do not want to see their children make decisions that are not in their best interest.

"A Muslim does not get stung from the same hole twice."(Prophet Muhammad -pbuh)

Your family members need the spiritual support you have to offer them. Therefore, please do not spend too much time feeling sorry for your self. When you reflect on the problems of love ones, you may ease your own self pity. Your brothers and sisters would love to get a letter from you, provided its' written from a position of strength.

Do not write your siblings singing the blues and complaining about the way you are treated. Your brothers, sisters and cousins know you. They probably warned you occasionally to "straighten up and fly right". We do not always listen.

Allah (God) is preparing you to help others. However, your heart must be right and you will be able to invite others to join in a life of peace and success through God's Grace. You are not to play yourself cheap during this "low point" in life. Allah is the final Judge and He and He alone determines who enters paradise and who enters the Hell Fire. Human beings are too quick to judge each other. You cannot determine the value of your fellow human being nor can he determine yours. Allah makes this determination.

"Oh Mankind! Reverence your Guardian Lord. Who created you from a single person and created of like nature, his mate, and from them twain scattered like seeds countless men and women. Fear Allah, through whom you demand your mutual rights, and reverence the wombs that bore you: for Allah ever watches over you."(Quran sura 4 ayatt 1 Nisa The Women)

Your mother may be an addict and a prostitute. She may be uneducated and mean spirited, or she may have punished you unjustly. You may have wished for your mothers' death before your birth. Your father too may have been brutal and abusive, or he may be an alcoholic. Regardless of what has happened in the past or how we may feel, Allah says that we are to "honor and respect our parents".